5-MINUTE
BLISS

5-MINUTE
BLISS

A More Joyful, Connected, and Fulfilled You
in Just 5 MINUTES A DAY

COURTNEY E. ACKERMAN

Adams Media
New York   London   Toronto   Sydney   New Delhi

Adams Media
An Imprint of Simon & Schuster, Inc.
57 Littlefield Street
Avon, Massachusetts 02322

First Adams Media trade paperback edition June 2019

ADAMS MEDIA and colophon are trademarks of Simon & Schuster.

For information about special discounts for bulk purchases, please contact Simon & Schuster Special Sales at 1-866-506-1949 or business@simonandschuster.com.

The Simon & Schuster Speakers Bureau can bring authors to your live event. For more information or to book an event contact the Simon & Schuster Speakers Bureau at 1-866-248-3049 or visit our website at www.simonspeakers.com.

Interior design by Michelle Kelly

Manufactured in the United States of America

10 9 8 7 6 5 4 3 2 1

Library of Congress Cataloging-in-Publication Data
Names: Ackerman, Courtney E.
Title: 5-minute bliss / Courtney E. Ackerman.
Description: Avon, Massachusetts:
Adams Media, 2019.
Series: 5-minute.
Identifiers: LCCN 2019001245 | ISBN 9781507210475 (pb) | ISBN 9781507210482 (ebook)
Subjects: LCSH: Self-actualization (Psychology) | Motivation (Psychology) | BISAC: SELF-HELP / Personal Growth / Happiness. | SELF-HELP / Motivational & Inspirational. | SELF-HELP / Personal Growth / Success.
Classification: LCC BF637.S4 A344 2019 | DDC 158.1--dc23
LC record available at https://lccn.loc.gov/2019001245

ISBN 978-1-5072-1047-5
ISBN 978-1-5072-1048-2 (ebook)

ACKNOWLEDGMENTS

I am sincerely grateful for all the love and support that allowed me to write this book. Thank you to each and every one of my family and friends who encouraged and motivated me.

Ben, thank you for being my biggest cheerleader and for always believing in me.

To Cal and Jeanne, my wonderful parents, thank you for teaching me how to work hard and keep at it, no matter what obstacles pop up.

To my brother Dillon, thank you for being my inspiration for portions of this book and for giving me your advice and your support.

Stacie Walker, thank you for encouraging me to advocate for myself and know my own worth.

Thank you to Ross Lallian, Evan Wallis, Destiny Ackerman, Raechel Russo, and Frank Ortega for celebrating every success with me.

Thank you to Jackie, Brett, and everyone else at Adams Media for providing the guidance, feedback, and support necessary to get this book from the first draft to the final.

I could not have done this without all of you, and you have my deepest gratitude.

CONTENTS

PART 3
**Experience Bliss in Your
Relationships 151**

11

INTRODUCTION

Bliss—that feeling of inner joy, happiness, and peace—can be an elusive goal in today's busy world. In order to meet all of your commitments, you can often overlook the importance of taking time for yourself and enjoying the things that make you happy—those things that make your life worth living!

Fortunately, *5-Minute Bliss* is here to help you regain your joy! In it you'll find more than two hundred quick and easy ways to discover a bit more bliss and incorporate it into your life. All you need is 5 minutes (or less) to relax, release the pressures of life, and find some joy. From practicing gratitude and embracing your individuality and creativity, to improving your relationships and finding peace in your surroundings, this book will be your guide to purposefully enjoying all the little moments in life and being the most authentic, happiest version of yourself.

These exercises don't require much time, effort, or other resources, and they are accessible to just about everyone! Flip to any page in this book and take just 5 minutes to boost your bliss, enhance your quality of life, and find new and improved ways to create and maintain your happiness. If you're looking for quick and easy ways to add a little more joy, peace, and bliss to your daily life, you've come to the right place!

PART 1

EXPERIENCE BLISS IN YOUR MIND

TREAT YOURSELF LIKE
YOU WOULD A DEAR FRIEND

Reframing your mind to think of yourself in a kinder way is an excellent first step toward inviting more bliss into your life. We generally have little trouble uplifting, encouraging, and cheering up a friend, but we sometimes struggle to do this for ourselves.

Practice treating yourself like a beloved friend or family member to open yourself up to a more blissful life.

Here's how to treat yourself like a friend:

1. Imagine that a friend is sharing her troubles with you, and they happen to be exactly the same as your own.
2. Think about how you would respond to this friend. Would you tell her "Too bad, so sad!" or would you offer a shoulder to lean on, words of encouragement, and assurances that she is loved and that she will make it through this?
3. Take the exact words, gestures, and compassion you would give to that friend and offer them to yourself.
4. Start to think of yourself as a friend. In truth, you are the one who knows you best, and you have the capacity to be the best friend you could ever have, so commit to acting like it!

LISTEN TO YOUR FAVORITE SONG

Music is such a wonderful tool for influencing our mood and shaping our experiences. Use this exercise to remind yourself just how powerful music really is.

Find a quiet spot or pull out your headphones if you're in a public place. Find one of your favorite songs—preferably one with an upbeat tone—and start listening.

As you listen to this much-loved song, think about three things:

1. How grateful you are for the ability to listen to music (if you are deaf or hard of hearing, read the lyrics to your favorite song or poem instead).
2. What this song brings up in your mind—a specific memory or perhaps a daydream or fantasy? Does it make you remember good times or look forward to new ones?
3. What the artists might have been thinking and feeling when they created this piece of art for you and all their other listeners.

Take time to appreciate the music and you'll get a nice little rush of bliss!

CONSIDER THE ROAD NOT TAKEN

In this exercise, you'll reflect on your past and find contentment and renewed joy in the choices you made.

Identify the two or three choices that you are the most proud of making, the ones you believe had the most significant impact on your life. These don't necessarily need to be the weightiest decisions—like the decision to propose to your significant other or take a new job across the country—they just need to be important moments in your life. For example, you might choose telling the truth in a moment when it mattered most or doing something kind for someone who ended up repaying the favor in a big way. Or perhaps you decided to stay home and help take care of a sick relative instead of moving away for an educational or career opportunity, and this decision allowed you to make meaningful connections you otherwise wouldn't have been able to make.

Using your 20/20 hindsight, think about how your life might have turned out if you hadn't taken those risks or made those good decisions. What would have happened if you had lied in that pivotal moment? Where would you be if you had taken that opportunity instead of staying to fulfill your familial responsibilities?

Consider where you would be right now, who you would be with, what you would be doing, and most important of all, whether you would be as happy and fulfilled as you are right now, in this moment.

Chances are, you would not be as happy if you hadn't made those decisions. Reflect on all the things that make you happy that you probably wouldn't get to enjoy if you had taken the other road—like your spouse, your current home, a job you enjoy—and find a sense of bliss and a feeling of joy in that reflection.

LIST YOUR STRENGTHS

A good way to get a boost of bliss is to work on feeling better about yourself. It's much easier to feel joyful when you feel good about yourself! If you have trouble feeling good about yourself—as many of us do from time to time—try directing your attention toward the best parts of you.

Follow these easy steps to get on your way to a happier you:

1. First, grab a pen and a piece of paper so you can record your strengths instead of just thinking about them in the moment.
2. Next, think about activities and tasks or chores that you do well, that you enjoy, and/or that you receive compliments on, and jot these down. Remember, there may be a lot of things that you are good at but hate doing. These are not strengths. A strength should be something that you have a passion or desire to do, something that makes you feel happy and strong inside.
3. Take a moment to think about what it is that makes you good at these things and write that trait or quality down; for example, if you find yourself finishing crossword puzzles in no time at all, then you might note that you are a good problem-solver or that you have a knack for language.

And voilà! You have a list of your strengths that you can refer to when you want to feel a little happier with yourself.

IDENTIFY YOUR SUPER STRENGTHS

For this exercise, you'll give yourself a mood boost by focusing on what you do best.

Follow these steps to identify your super strengths:

1. Come up with a list of your personal strengths (e.g., creativity, organization, meeting new people). If you haven't already identified your personal strengths, take a few minutes to do so. The exercise "List Your Strengths" can help you come up with a list if you need some inspiration.
2. Once you have a list of about eight to ten strengths, think about how much you use each one on a regular basis. Consider what is a "super" strength (something you are exceptionally good at) and what is a more moderate strength.
3. Reorder your strengths into a list that starts with your top strength and ends with the strength you feel is your least or bottom strength.

Now you have an ordered list of your strengths to remind you that you are competent, capable, and talented. Refer back to this list if you need a boost of happiness or self-appreciation and remember that your unique mix of strengths makes you a valuable person with a lot to contribute to the world.

AFFIRM YOURSELF!

Affirmations are simple statements about yourself that you can repeat whenever you need a boost of energy, motivation, happiness, or peace.

First, you'll need to come up with some affirmations. Follow these easy guidelines to come up with some killer affirmations:

1. Make your affirmation short and sweet; it shouldn't be longer than one short sentence, and it should focus on just one idea (e.g., "I am a good person," not "I am a good person who is talented at basketball, skillful in my craft, and an excellent father").
2. Make sure it is worded in the here and now (in this exact moment, at this very spot).
3. Make it a positive statement about yourself that represents what you want to be, what you hope to be, and what you know you are capable of in the near future.

Here are a few examples to help you get started:

- I am a kind and generous person.
- I have valuable talents and skills to offer.
- I am a good [choose a role like daughter, sister, friend, spouse, or mother].
- I am an excellent listener for my friends and family.

- I am worthy of the love and affection I receive.
- I can accomplish any goal that I set my mind to accomplishing.

Once you have a list of a few positive, present-tense, and uplifting affirmations, it's time to start practicing! Repeat them right away to get off to a good start, and plan out at least a couple 5-minute periods throughout your day when you can repeat them again.

Taking just a few minutes out of your busy day to reaffirm that you are a good person, loveable, worthy of respect, and so on, can end up making all the difference in how you feel about yourself and the choices you make. Start practicing affirmations today and you'll feel an instant boost of bliss in your life!

START A DAILY JOURNAL

If you're not already journaling, you really should give it a try. Spending just a few minutes each day journaling can help you in so many ways, and it couldn't be easier to get started. Grab a journal and follow these guidelines:

1. Open your journal and write the date at the top of the page.
2. Take a minute or two to think about how your day has gone so far. Think about what has happened, how you felt about it then, how you feel about it now, and your thought patterns throughout the day.
3. Write it down!

It really is that easy. If you find you are having trouble thinking of what to say or fearing the blank page, try these tips:

- **Find fun journal prompts.** There are whole books on journal prompts, or you can find them online.
- **Free write.** Take your 5 minutes and just write down whatever comes into your head. Sure, it may not be the most insightful writing you've ever done, but you also may be surprised by what you come up with when you open the gates.

- **Don't limit yourself to words.** Remember, this journal is yours to use as you wish, so if you feel like drawing, doodling, pasting in pressed flowers, taping in ticket stubs, or whatever, then go for it!

Journaling is a quick and easy activity that can help you organize your thoughts, make sense of what happens to you and how you react to it, and dive deeper into recognizing your own patterns, habits, and tendencies. The simple act of writing can be a blissful release of creative energy, and clearing your head leaves more room for contentment and joy.

CREATE YOUR OWN ODE TO JOY

If you're not a poet by nature, don't worry! You don't need to write *good* poetry for this exercise to work; you only need to write authentically and from the heart.

First, start out by taking a few minutes to reflect on the experience of joy. Think about what it feels like when you are joyful. Ask yourself questions like:

- Does your heart beat faster or slower?
- Does your mind slow down or speed up?
- How does your body feel when you are full of joy?
- What emotions often go hand in hand with joy?

Once you have a good idea of what it feels like for you to experience joy, start putting together your piece. Use your answers to the previous questions to come up with a work that you could use to describe your experience of joy for someone else. You can think of it as a poem, a song, or simply a string of words and phrases that accurately capture your personal experience of joy.

Just spending time thinking about being joyful will encourage you to *be* joyful, and now you'll have a happy reminder you can read whenever you want to recapture that feeling!

SHOW YOURSELF SOME LOVE

A surefire way to boost your bliss is to extend love to the person you have the most reason to love: you!

Loving yourself is the first step along the way to true happiness, because true happiness is only possible if you come from a place of clarity and acceptance about who you are. To open the door to bliss for yourself, work on improving your self-love. Give this simple exercise a try to get started.

Wherever you are and whatever you're in the middle of doing, press the metaphorical pause button. Ask yourself how you're feeling right now, in this very moment. Are you feeling happy? Sad? Stressed out? Nothing in particular?

Whatever term describes your current feelings, tell yourself it's okay to feel that way. There's nothing wrong with feeling however you feel. Offer yourself some acceptance, some compassion, and some love. If it helps, give yourself an actual hug to emphasize the love!

DESIGN YOUR PERFECT DAY

We are busy people—busier than ever in our modern, fast-paced world—and we rarely have time to take an entire day to simply indulge and enjoy ourselves. Luckily, you don't need an entire day to get a little boost of bliss! All you need is a few minutes to plan out your perfect day.

Sit down with a pen and a piece of paper and think about how you would spend your time if you had an entire day of freedom: no work, no school, and no responsibilities.

Outline exactly how you would spend this day. For example, you might write:

- Sleep in until 9 a.m.
- Eat at my favorite brunch spot.
- See a movie with a good friend.
- Curl up in the window seat and read for an hour.
- Take a long, relaxing walk with my spouse/SO.
- Make dinner together and share a bottle of wine.
- Host a game night with friends.
- Head to bed around 11 p.m.

You'll find that just planning your perfect day can give you a bit of the joy that actually living it would!

PRACTICE MINDFULNESS

Mindfulness is a wonderful tool. It can help you feel calmer, more focused, more relaxed, happier, and just all-around healthier. As it turns out, it can also make you more blissful!

If you've never engaged in mindfulness before, this exercise is a great way to ease into it and familiarize yourself with the practice.

1. **Find a comfortable spot to sit or lie down—but not too comfy!** You don't want to fall asleep in the middle of your practice.
2. **Settle in and close your eyes.** Shut your mind down as you shut your eyes, and let go of any sense of rigid control over your thoughts.
3. **Allow your thoughts to come and go, your mind drifting from one to the next.** Don't stop and focus on any of them, but don't avoid or ignore any of them either. As they pass, do your best to consider them without any value judgment (e.g., "I shouldn't feel this way" or "Wow, what a terrible thought to have!").
4. **Spend a few minutes simply allowing your thoughts to pass in and out of your mind.** If you find your mind wandering off on a tangent, simply direct it gently back to its objective and nonjudgmental state.
5. **If it helps, you can focus on your breathing.** Feel each breath as it enters your lungs, fills your chest, and slowly escapes through your

nose. Don't try to control it, just observe it and pay attention to how it feels to breathe.

6. **When you're ready to end your practice, simply bring your awareness back to your surroundings and let go of any lingering thoughts.** Allow your eyes to flutter open, and go on with your day as planned, but with one caveat—try to carry your relaxed and mindful state along with you.

Congratulations, you practiced mindfulness! You'll find that this practice is an excellent way to feel peaceful, relaxed, and even blissful. Do it regularly for best results.

PRACTICE OPTIMISM

Research shows that optimistic people are happier, healthier, and more successful than pessimists. You probably already knew that, but did you know that you can become more optimistic by practicing?

Try this exercise to cultivate a more optimistic outlook:

1. Think about something big, nerve-racking, or important coming up soon.
2. Write down all the scenarios in your head in which something goes wrong at this big event.
3. For each scenario, write down three alternative scenarios—how things could go *right* instead of wrong. They should be related to the "wrong" scenario. For example, if you're worried about making a fool of yourself on a date, note that you and your date might both do something silly and share a laugh over it. Each scenario should be realistic and believable.
4. Continue listing three ways things could go "right" for every "wrong" until you've run out of "wrong" scenarios.

This exercise allows you to practice coming up with at least three positive thoughts for each negative one. The more you practice thinking positive thoughts, the more normal and natural it will become.

REMEMBER YOUR PAST

Taking a few minutes to reflect on your past is a healthy practice and a good way to make you feel more joyful. No matter who you are or where you've been, you have some fond memories to look back on.

1. Think about your happiest memories and come up with a list of four or five.
2. Think about each of these memories in turn, focusing on what it felt like to be that happy. Try to re-create that feeling inside you.
3. For each memory, write down one word that best captures how you felt in the moment. For example, if one of your happiest memories was graduating from college, you might write "Proud."
4. Once you have selected a word for each memory, look at the list and read it out loud to yourself. Think about how wonderful it is that you are able to feel such wonderful feelings, remind yourself that you deserve to feel these feelings, and be grateful that you have experienced them.

VISUALIZE YOUR FUTURE

You know that feeling when you're really, really looking forward to something in your near future? It might be something like going on a vacation or seeing a loved one you haven't seen in a while. Whatever it is, you can't wait for the moment to arrive!

That anticipation and excitement for our future push us to be happy in the present. We don't always have a good reason to be giddy about the future, but this exercise can help you find one.

First, take a minute or two to think about what you want your future to look like. Narrow it down to one single moment. You don't need to know every detail, but you should have at least a vague idea of a moment in your future that makes you happy. Your moment might be cradling a newborn child with your proud and happy spouse, getting your first book published, or receiving an award or recognition of some kind.

Having just one realistic, happy potential moment to look forward to—no matter how far away—can help you to be more joyful and hopeful in the present.

SAY A QUICK PRAYER/TALK TO THE UNIVERSE

Prayer can have some incredible positive effects on our lives. Whether prayers are "answered" or not, the simple act of praying itself usually leaves us calmer, happier, and more blissful than we were before.

And it's not only prayer—meditating, practicing mindfulness, or any form of communication with a "higher power" can all lead to the same outcomes.

All you need to do is come up with something to say to the universe, God, or your higher power of choice. If you consider yourself religious or spiritual, you likely won't have a problem coming up with a prayer!

If you do have trouble, try sending this quick thought out into the universe:

"I am alive, I am whole, I am present, and I am grateful for these gifts."

It's that simple! Give it a shot—saying even a brief prayer (and really meaning what you say) is a quick ticket to a more blissful mood.

REMIND YOURSELF OF THE GOOD

It can be easy to forget just how wonderful life is, but luckily it can be just as easy to remember the wonders of life—with a little nudge. When you stop and think about it, you'll see that there really is so much to be grateful for, to be inspired by, and to revel in!

If you're feeling distracted by bad news and negative events, stop and take a moment to remind yourself of "the good." This includes things that make you feel joyful, blissful, inspired, proud, optimistic, hopeful, elevated, or just plain happy.

List your favorite things, think of inspiring stories you've read, and recall your own memories of kindness, bravery, and compassion. Remind yourself of the best things in life and reflect on the incredible acts of goodness that people are capable of. Examples from your own life are most powerful in boosting your bliss, but don't worry if you can't come up with enough good things to focus on. There's lots of good news out there if you look for it!

If you find it exceptionally difficult to come up with a laundry list of good things from your own life or the lives of your friends and loved ones, check your local paper or scour the Internet for a recent news story about someone doing an extraordinarily good deed, read a poem by an inspirational author, or listen to a song that you find uplifting— whatever works to remind you of the good.

Making time to think about the good things in life instead of dwelling on the bad will help you see all that there is to be joyful about, and this can be a bigger boost to your bliss than just about any other exercise! Isn't it amazing how powerful our brains can be in terms of influencing our mood?

TRY A MORNING JOURNAL SESSION

Most people write in their journals at night, but making an early morning entry can have its own unique focus and benefits. Some of the benefits of journaling in the morning include:

- **You start the day on a positive note.** Try writing about something you are grateful for each morning and you'll notice that this sense of gratitude makes your day a little brighter.
- **It gets you aligned with your goals.** Writing about your goals and dreams each morning helps keep you focused on those goals all day long.
- **It focuses your mind and helps get rid of the clutter.** Writing down all your thoughts in the morning helps get them out of your mind and allows you to be able to focus on the important things.

Give morning journaling a try by following these guidelines:

- **Focus on the day ahead.** Journaling often covers what has already happened since it usually occurs at the end of the day; with a morning journal session, you will spend most of your time thinking about the day to come.
- **Write about what you *expect* will happen today.** Do you have anything in particular coming up today? A presentation at work, a date night, or an important meeting?

- **Write about what you hope will happen today.** How do you want that presentation, date night, or meeting to go?

By focusing on the near future, some realistic outcomes, and some hoped-for outcomes, you will get some good practice being more forward-looking and optimistic but realistic. If you already journal regularly, try a morning journal session at least once or twice a week.

QUOTE YOUR FAVORITE COMEDY

When you're feeling low, sometimes an action as simple as remembering or referencing your favorite movie or TV show can give you the mood boost you need to go on with your day.

To take advantage of the opportunity to spike your mood, follow these steps:

1. Think of your favorite funny TV show or movie in the comedy genre.
2. Think of a few of your favorite lines from the show or movie. Write them down if it helps you keep them in mind.
3. Read over them and remember the funny, silly, or otherwise enjoyable moments in which these lines were delivered. If you can restage the scene in your head, you can get an extra dose of funny!
4. Keep these in mind as you go about your day and pull out one of these quotes when the moment is just right. Stay alert—the right moment will come!

This exercise is a "twofer" because it will not only make you feel happier, but it will probably make someone else laugh too!

GIVE YOURSELF A BREAK

We often get so caught up in our day-to-day worries and tasks that we can forget to give ourselves a little time to breathe.

Do yourself a favor and take a break from it all—and I mean *all* of it. Find a quiet spot to sit or go outside to enjoy the outdoors and simply take 5 minutes to do nothing. Switch off, allow your mind to wander, and simply don't do anything at all. If it helps, imagine yourself as your own strict, by-the-book sort of boss. When the boss (i.e., you) says it's time to take a break, it's time to take a break! There's no arguing with the boss.

If it sounds like a super easy exercise, that's because it is—what other exercise calls for you to sit and do nothing? However, that doesn't mean there aren't some helpful guidelines you can follow to make the experience a positive and effective one:

- **Minimize any potential disruptions or distractions;** this might mean turning your phone on silent, walking away from busy areas, or putting on some noise-canceling headphones. If you do decide to use headphones, avoid listening to music or anything else that could be distracting; the point is to mute the hustle and bustle around you and to discourage others who may be thinking about interrupting your break time.

- **Turn off your inner critic; don't let any voice saying,** "You should really be working on Task A" or "Aren't you worried about Concern B?" break in. For the purposes of this exercise, you are your own boss, and the boss says it's break time. When you're on break, you don't have to think about any of that!
- **Aside from the two previous guidelines, do whatever you want!** Want to meditate? Great! Want to sit and daydream? Do it! Feel like staring into empty space for 5 minutes? Go for it!

Taking just 5 minutes to do nothing can be surprisingly effective in making you calmer, cooler, and more content.

CHALLENGE YOUR INNER CRITIC

One of the best things you can do for yourself is to get hold of your inner critic. We all have one, that small voice in the back of your mind that plays off your worst anxieties, causing you to question your worth. Some people's inner critics are stronger than others', but we have all at one time or another faced that inability to ward off internal criticisms. You don't need to completely silence this nitpicky voice; you just need to know when to listen to it and when (and how) to tell it to shut up.

This exercise is best practiced when your inner critic is loud and obnoxious, since that's when it's easy to catch. When your inner critic pops up, try this:

1. Identify the things your inner critic is saying and the things that are coming from the authentic "you."
2. Take what the inner critic says under advisement; consider whether it's right in any respects or if it's way off base this time. If it helps, feel free to make a list, write in your journal, or take some notes.
3. Address your inner critic gently and compassionately. Try saying, "Inner Critic, I know you're worried about X, but you really don't need to be. Here's my plan for dealing with X... We're going to be fine."

Remember that your inner critic is a part of you and though it is often misguided, it's trying to look out for your best interests. Treat it with care and you'll see it begin to soften.

SING YOUR HEART OUT

You don't need to be good at something to enjoy doing it. Singing is a prime example of this! Lots of us love to belt out our favorite tunes (whether in front of a crowd at karaoke or alone in the shower), but we're under no illusion that we'll be winning a singing competition anytime soon.

For this exercise, you don't need to be good at singing—you just need to enjoy doing it!

To get an instant boost of bliss, blast your favorite song in the car or shower and sing along to it. Don't worry about what you sound like or how you look; just let yourself sink into the song and give it all your energy for a few minutes.

Singing can be so enjoyable because you engage with your breath, with your body, and with your creativity, in addition to connecting with positive memories and good feelings through your favorite songs. Take advantage of this unique experience by singing with all your heart!

WHAT I LIKE ABOUT ME

For this exercise, you're going to come up with a list of things you like about yourself. If that sounds scary, you're not alone! It can be difficult for us to get real and get positive about ourselves, but all it takes is a little practice.

Have you ever tried listing the things you love about someone in order to cheer them up? Now it's time you repay the favor—to yourself!

This is most impactful when you're feeling a bit down about yourself, but it can help anytime you want a little surge of good feelings.

Grab a piece of paper or a notebook and something to write with and follow these instructions:

1. **Think about yourself from the perspective of your partner, your best friend, or a beloved family member.** It can be really difficult to find the right balance, but try to come up with neutral and objective thoughts while maintaining a warm and friendly attitude toward yourself. You want to come up with some accurate strengths and features you appreciate about yourself, but you also want to take a kindly perspective rather than a completely cold and detached one.
2. **Identify at least five things you like about yourself.** One or two can be superficial, but try to focus on qualities, traits, and habits. For example, you might list your eyes, your sense of humor, your work

ethic, your fashion sense, and your commitment to helping those less fortunate.

3. **Think about how much you appreciate friends and family with these good traits,** and tell yourself what you would say to cheer them up or make them feel a little more positive about themselves.

Identifying what you like about yourself can be hard—especially if you're feeling really low—but it's one of the best things you can do for yourself!

WAKE UP WITH AFFIRMATIONS

Affirmations can be a great way to help you get through a difficult time, but they can also help you as you go about your regular daily routine. If you have a habit of forgetting to practice your affirmations during your busy day, committing to a morning practice might be just the thing for you.

Make sure to come up with some affirmations ahead of time; just remember that they should:

1. Be positively worded.
2. Be in the present tense.
3. Make you feel good about yourself.

To practice creating affirmations, see the "Affirm Yourself!" exercise earlier in this part.

When practicing affirmations in the morning, try to run through them as soon as possible after you wake up. That could be in bed right after you turn off your alarm, or it might be as soon as you head into the bathroom to brush your teeth.

Here are some examples:

- Every day I discover new and interesting paths to pursue.
- I am focused on my goals and feel passionate about my work.
- I have everything I need to face the obstacles that may appear.

- I am living to my full potential.
- I choose to think positively today.
- I am grateful for this day and all its many blessings.
- This day is another opportunity to grow and improve.

Whenever you get to it, just make sure to say each one of them aloud and to say it with feeling! Affirmations work best when you put in solid effort to say them like you mean them.

TUCK YOURSELF IN WITH AFFIRMATIONS

If morning affirmations aren't your thing, evening affirmations might be the way to go. Although saying your affirmations in the morning can get you off to a good start for the day to come, it can be just as important to make sure you prepare for a peaceful and restful night.

When you're getting ready for bed, take a few minutes to stand in front of the mirror and repeat your affirmations to your reflection. Make sure to:

1. Look yourself in the eyes.
2. Say your affirmations out loud.
3. Believe them!

That last part might take some practice, but that's why we say affirmations more than once.

Here are some examples:

- I release the worry, fear, and anxiety of today and my mind is calm.
- I am grateful for today and the lessons it has brought.
- I have done my best today and earned this rest.
- I am happy with what I have accomplished today.
- I am looking forward to tomorrow and the opportunities it brings.
- This sleep will refresh me for a new and exciting day tomorrow.

- I can rest knowing that everything I need is coming.
- I can rest deeply and fully and awake refreshed.

When you're finished, hop into bed and repeat them once more, either aloud or in your head. If you can, use them as a sort of lullaby to drift off to sleep. Going to bed with positive, happy thoughts will lead to positive, happy dreams and a more blissful morning, so give it a shot!

MAKE A GRATITUDE LIST

Remembering all the good things in your life is one of the best ways to enhance your bliss. When you take the time to notice what you have, it is much easier to choose to be grateful for it.

Boost your gratitude—and your bliss—by making a list of all the things for which you are grateful. To get started, follow these steps:

1. Take out your journal or notebook and open it up to a fresh page.
2. Kick off your list with the big things: your home (whether you own, rent, or are just "crashing" at the moment), your health (even if it's not the very best), your relationships with any/all loved ones, your job, and so on.
3. Continue your list by ticking off the things you might not think about as often: your neighborhood, the air quality where you live, the availability of fresh drinking water, your ability to get around and provide for yourself, and so on.
4. Next, write down the people you are grateful for and a brief note on why you are grateful for them. For example, you might write "Greg, for loving me unconditionally" or "Mom, for always being there for me when I need her."
5. Finally, make sure to think a bit more deeply about some of the things you are grateful for: your sense of humor, any special talents

or skills you have, being born in the circumstances that made you who you are, and your ability to be grateful in the first place.

Make the list as long and comprehensive as you can in 5 minutes, but don't feel constrained to *just* 5 minutes. You can always return to the list later! Once you've got a good, long list of things you are grateful for, keep it in your back pocket (physically or metaphorically) and take it out when you're feeling down or need a little boost of bliss.

CREATE A BLISS MANTRA

Mantras are similar to affirmations but are not quite the same. Affirmations are positive statements about who you are right here and right now, while mantras are simply words, phrases, or statements that help you stay focused, mindful, and in the right frame of mind.

To create your own bliss mantra, come up with something you can repeat to yourself during your day. It should:

1. Remind you of your intention to be more blissful.
2. Be short and sweet.
3. Be easy to remember and repeat.
4. Make you smile!

Your mantra can be one or two essentially meaningless syllables or it can be made of words or phrases that are intensely, personally significant to you. Whatever works for you is a good mantra!

When you create your mantra, stay mindful of your intention and pour that intention into it; you want it to be a good reminder to stay open and invite bliss into each moment.

Once you have your mantra ready to go, remember to use it often!

GIVE YOURSELF A COMPLIMENT

Everyone likes compliments. They're fun to give and great to receive, especially when they're heartfelt and sincere. Unfortunately, you can't get heartfelt, sincere compliments on demand from other people!

That's why you need to practice complimenting yourself. Compliments from yourself are the best compliments in some ways, since you know exactly what you need to hear in the moment.

To give yourself a boost of bliss, try complimenting yourself.

Stand in front of a mirror and look yourself in the eyes. Think about the one thing you would love to hear right now. Do you need a boost of confidence about your looks? Or perhaps you're feeling low about your performance at work?

Whatever you need a boost in, focus on that and pay yourself a compliment that follows three guidelines:

1. It must be positive and well-intentioned.
2. It must be sincere and genuine.
3. It must make you feel good!

Give yourself a sincere compliment whenever you want to feel happier and more blissful.

REFLECT ON YOUR LIFE

Engaging in reflection is a healthy way to make sure you have perspective, stay grounded, and identify any potentially troublesome thought patterns or habits; however, it can also be an excellent way to find a little extra bliss!

To give reflection a try, find someplace quiet and comfortable where you can sit and think. Try to be still and relax, both in mind and body. Breathe slowly and regularly, allowing your thoughts to slowly drift through your mind without trying to control them.

When you feel centered and ready to begin, direct your attention to three areas:

1. Your personal values.
2. Your goals and aspirations in life.
3. How your values and goals align.

Think about how your values and goals fit into your life. Ask yourself whether your regular daily activities reflect your values and whether they contribute to your goals. If you find any incongruence, think about how you can fix it.

Check in and reflect often to keep your life in alignment. When you live your life in a way that is congruent with your values and goals, you open yourself up to experiencing bliss daily.

DRAW A PICTURE

You already know that a picture is worth a thousand words, but you might not know that it can also bring you a thousand happy thoughts!

Okay, that might be an exaggeration, but it's true that drawing something blissful can give you that same sense of bliss.

For this exercise, you don't need to be an artist. In fact, it might even be more impactful if you don't draw often.

First, think of a happy image. It could be scenery, like rolling hills or a flower-filled meadow. It could be something near and dear to you, like your spouse's perfume or cologne bottle. It might even be something else entirely, like a shiny balloon on a string or a road sign for a place that is meaningful to you.

Once you have the image in mind, take a few minutes to sketch it out. It doesn't matter what tools you use to draw it or how technically "good" it is. The only thing that matters is that the image imparts some of its bliss to you as you draw.

When you finish, gaze at your picture and absorb every ounce of bliss it represents.

CREATE A TO-DO LIST

You know how you always have that mental list of things you'd like to do, but you never seem to get around to them? It's time to make it official!

Grab a pen and a pad or notebook and flip to a fresh sheet of paper. Write "My To-Do List" at the top, and start writing some of those nebulous tasks and half-finished ideas down on paper.

Often, just getting your "to-dos" out of your head and into a list will give you a little injection of happiness and perhaps a bit of relief as well. It's hard to try to juggle everything in your head, which is why recording some of those swirling thoughts and ideas can do you good.

However, if you want to really make an impact on your mood and clear your head, try any of these suggestions:

- **At the top of your list, include several to-dos you have recently finished and cross them off.** This can give you a wonderful sense of accomplishment and confidence in your ability to continue knocking them out, one by one.
- **After you write them down, organize them according to importance.** Put the to-do that is most important to you at the top and the least important one at the bottom.
- **Categorize them by domain.** Keep your work-related to-dos in one list, your home maintenance/improvement to-dos in another, and your family- and friend-related to-dos in a third list.

- **Categorize them by effort required and come up with some sort of symbol or color code to tell them apart.** This will help you feel even more satisfied when you cross off the big ones!
- **Set a goal to complete each to-do by a certain date and organize them chronologically.** That way, you can cross one off and jump directly to the next one.

Try one of these suggestions—or all five of them—to get a boost of bliss and satisfaction. Just remember to follow through on them!

CROSS ONE THING OFF YOUR TO-DO LIST

There are many ways to create a to-do list for yourself, so find one that works for you, whether it's a handwritten list on the fridge, a note in your phone, a reminder app, or a Post-it note on your desk. All you need is a quick list of the things you need to accomplish today.

After you have your to-do list filled out and ready to go (if you don't, see the earlier exercise titled "Create a To-Do List"), pick one thing that you can do right away or pretty much right away.

Outline what you'll need to cross this item off your list and any steps you need to take before completing this to-do item.

Now, the important part—go out and do it! Even if it doesn't take very long to complete or if you feel silly for doing it, make sure to embrace your hard work and thank yourself for your dedication to working through your to-do list.

Give yourself a virtual "pat on the back" (or a real one, if you can reach!) for tackling one of the many things you aimed to do in the near future. In fact, if this was a to-do that has been hanging over your head for a while, then go ahead and build in a reward for yourself for getting it done. Not only will that give you the bliss of having accomplished the task, but it will also add a little bliss from a small, well-deserved treat.

Take a deep breath and allow the satisfaction and fulfillment of crossing one thing off your to-do list turn into a deep and fulfilling sense of bliss.

COLOR A SCENE IN AN ADULT COLORING BOOK

I know, I know—it sounds silly! But many people have found adult coloring books to be soothing, enjoyable, and even bliss-inducing. It might not work for you, but you might as well give it a try, right?

Buy an adult coloring book from the store. If you'd rather not go searching for one, you can always go online to download some free coloring sheets.

Grab some crayons or colored pencils and let your inner child out to play! Color inside the lines, color outside the lines, make it look realistic, or make it as exotic and surreal as you'd like—however you feel like doing it is fine.

As you color, let yourself remember what it felt like to be a kid. Remind yourself of how great it felt to be carefree and full of joy as a default setting. Allow some of that untarnished joy in life to seep into you and fill you up.

For an added bit of bliss, remember that a glass of wine makes a great companion to an adult coloring book!

TAKE A PHOTO OF SOMETHING MEANINGFUL

Many of us are very comfortable taking pictures with a smartphone and are not at all shy about documenting just about every piece of our lives, but some of us are slow to adapt to the new way of life.

If you are one of the latter type of people, and you often find yourself cursing your tendency to forget your camera or regretting your reluctance to drag out your phone for a good picture, this exercise is for you!

Follow these steps to snap a good picture *and* give yourself a boost of bliss:

1. Decide on your subject for the photograph. Popular subjects are things that remind you of those you love, like your child's drawings on the fridge or your dog's leash hanging by the door.
2. Whatever you pick, take a moment to arrange it for the most "artsy" look (i.e., whatever looks best to you). For instance, you might rearrange the magnets on your fridge and make the drawings slightly off-kilter instead of arranged in straight, strict-looking right angles.
3. Make sure the background of the photo isn't messy, chaotic, or embarrassing—think about all those photos people take in their bathrooms that end up showing something very personal or revealing in the background!

4. Make sure the lighting is good on your subject; it shouldn't be too bright or too dark, and it shouldn't be uneven.
5. Aim the camera and frame the perfect shot, but make sure it really is the "perfect" shot!
6. Take two or three pictures. You shouldn't need to take more than a couple of pictures if you put a lot of care into building the perfect photo in the first five steps.

Print the photo out and frame it for your desk or save it as your desktop background to get a mini boost of bliss every time you see it.

VISUALIZE YOUR HEART AS A FLOWER

If you have never practiced visualization before, this is an excellent exercise to get you started. Visualization can help you bring yourself into a calmer and more collected state, bring you more joy, and even boost your motivation.

In this visualization exercise, you'll envision your heart as a flower. Follow these steps to give yourself a bliss infusion:

1. Sit somewhere quiet and close your eyes.
2. See yourself in your mind's eye. Locate your heart within your body and look *through* your body to your heart.
3. Imagine that it is a tightly closed flower bud, just waiting to burst open. Notice what color, shape, texture, and type the flower bud is.
4. Breathe. As you inhale through your nose, imagine inhaling only good things—joy, meaning, love, respect, inspiration, and bliss.
5. As you inhale all these good things, imagine your heart flower opening. As you draw in more and more of the good things in life, watch your heart unfold and blossom like a flower.
6. Exhale and watch it blossom even more. Repeat the inhales and exhales as you visualize your heart opening up to the good like a flower in bloom.

TRY SOMETHING NEW

Forgive the cliché, but it's true: variety is the spice of life! Without variety, our days would turn into one big blur—one follows another, with little to distinguish them aside from marking them off on the calendar. With variety, we find excitement, exhilaration, and joy in our lives!

One excellent way to ensure that you keep your life open to bliss is to try something new. It doesn't need to be something big or bold; sometimes just branching out a tiny bit can be enough to keep things feeling fresh and exciting.

If there's something you've wanted to do for a while, and you can do it in just a few minutes, give it a shot! If nothing comes to mind, try one of these easy suggestions:

- Take a walk to an area of your neighborhood you haven't checked out before.
- Order takeout or delivery from a new restaurant.
- Try to take an artsy photograph.
- Create a unique and complex doodle.
- Listen to three new songs, each from a different genre.
- Try to create a new look with the makeup you already have.
- Visit a nearby museum or gallery that you've never been to.
- Say hello to a neighbor you don't usually talk to.

- Try cooking a new recipe.
- Make a photo album out of the photos you took on a recent trip instead of letting those photos get lost on your phone or computer.

See, it's not so hard to come up with something new to try—just use a little bit of imagination.

LIST YOUR WINS

It's empowering to know that you can be your own biggest cheer-leader. We often forget that, but it's true—no one knows exactly how to inspire and motivate and encourage you like yourself!

To try your hand at being your own cheerleader and bringing your own bliss into your life, list your wins.

Listing your wins is simply documenting some of your most impres-sive achievements, most valued accomplishments, and anything else you are proud of.

To get started, come up with a list of some of your biggest ones; think graduating from high school or college, securing your first "real" job, winning any kind of award, getting published, having your signifi-cant other accept your proposal, and so on. Write down anything that you are really proud of yourself for doing or that your family and friends might list as an accomplishment.

Next, think about some of the more basic ones that you might not think of as big accomplishments because lots of people can list them, like getting recognition for longevity at your work, making your car payment on time every month, buying a house, or completing a half-marathon. It doesn't matter how many other people have the same accomplishments under their belt—if it took more than a little effort, count it as a win.

Finally, get creative and think of all the wins that aren't even wins to you but normal, everyday functions; for example, it's a win if you get out of bed every morning and go to work—even though that may be the last thing you want to do. It's also a win if you manage to keep your children alive, clothed, fed, and at least relatively happy every day.

Let this exercise remind you of how many truly impressive and difficult things you accomplish all the time, and use the sense of fulfillment and bliss to encourage you to keep it up!

LIST YOUR WISHES

If you want to cultivate a steady and present sense of bliss in your life, you need to make sure that you have goals to work toward and things to look forward to. To lead a life that is conducive to bliss, try listing your wishes.

You can do this in your head, but it's best to record them somewhere, like your journal, a phone app, or even a random scrap of paper.

Create your list by writing down the things that really drive you, excite you, or get you fired up. For example:

- What do you want to happen in your future?
- What would your dream job be?
- Do you hope to win a Nobel Prize?
- Where have you always wanted to travel to?
- Have you always dreamed of starting your own business?
- Do you want to lose some weight?
- What would your dream house look like?
- What is your perfect mate like?

Whatever you desire most, write it down. It doesn't matter if it seems far-fetched or if you feel like it will take way too much effort to get there; your goals and wishes *should* stretch and challenge you.

Now that you have a list of your wishes, you can use it in tons of other bliss-boosting exercises, like setting specific and attainable goals, crossing things off your to-do list, and eventually listing some of your wishes as your wins!

SIGN UP TO VOLUNTEER

It takes more than a few minutes to volunteer and truly make a difference, but you can set yourself up for success (and bliss!) in the near future by signing up or otherwise committing to volunteer.

Find an organization that you like or that really speaks to you and your values. If you're an animal lover, the local shelter might be a good option. If you're passionate about at-risk youth, find a big brother/big sister or similar mentoring program. If you have family members or friends who have struggled with homelessness, find a local soup kitchen.

Whichever organization you pick, look online or call to find out about opportunities to volunteer. If you can sign up online, do it. If you can commit to volunteering at a certain time and place over the phone, do it.

Simply deciding to spend some of your time giving to others and contributing to a good cause will fill you with bliss—just make sure you follow through on it and get an even bigger payoff of bliss!

MAKE A DECISION YOU'VE BEEN PUTTING OFF

If you tend to overthink things or procrastinate, you know that making one seemingly simple decision can be time-consuming and stressful; however, you also know how good it feels to finally make one of those decisions!

To get your own rush of post-decision-making bliss, follow these simple steps:

1. **Bring to mind a decision you've been thinking about for a while.** Get some bonus bliss points by picking one that needs to be made ASAP!
2. **Think through it.** Whether this involves making a pro and con list, scouring the Internet, phoning a friend to talk about it, or anything else, just take a few minutes to really dig into it.
3. **Based on what you learned in step 2,** come up with the best outcome for this situation and make the decision that is most likely to bring this outcome to fruition.
4. **Finally, take one solid step—even if it's a tiny step—**to make the decision real. Tell someone about it, make the first move toward the path you've decided on, or purchase something you will use based on the decision you made.

Thank yourself for making the decision and enjoy the feeling of bliss it brings!

CREATE A MINI VISION BOARD

Vision boards are excellent tools to help you solidify your dreams and make your goals seem closer and more achievable than ever. This feeling of being competent enough to accomplish your goals carries a lot of other good feelings with it.

To make a mini vision board, follow these steps:

1. **Grab a piece of card stock, cardboard, or another sturdy background for your mini vision board.** It shouldn't be more than about a foot on each side.

2. **Get some images that represent your most desired goal** (if you're not certain about your long-term goals, try the "Set SMART Goals" exercise later in this part). You can draw these, download them from the Internet, cut them out of magazines, or grab some old photos.

3. **Arrange the images to correspond to your goals.** For example, if your goal is to backpack across Europe, you might have some images of backpacks, popular destinations in Europe, travelers, or beautiful scenery.

4. **Optional:** Add some color, glitter, ribbon, or any other type of embellishment to make your vision board visually appealing.

Hang it where you will see it often and let it bring you bliss and inspiration every time it catches your eye!

GIVE YOURSELF SOME GRATITUDE

For many of us, it's easier to show others gratitude than to show ourselves gratitude. That's common, but it's not something that is unchangeable; you can learn to be more grateful for everything, including yourself. More gratitude leads to greater bliss, so it's worth a shot!

To get started, think about some of the things you have accomplished that you may have never thought you could. If you have completed the "List Your Wins" exercise earlier in this part, this list is a good jumping-off point.

For each accomplishment, think about how much time and effort you invested in order to complete it. Chances are, each one took quite a bit of time and effort!

When you do great or challenging things, you have the option to view that as a wonderful gift you are giving to yourself. Embrace that option and thank yourself for all your hard work!

If you feel it would help, go ahead and treat yourself to something special as a sign of your gratitude.

PLAY A GAME

Think about how often you see children playing games. If you have young children at home, this is probably a common sight! Children are naturally playful, curious, eager to learn new things, and at least a little competitive, which leads them to a built-in love of games.

Now think back to when *you* played games as a child. You probably really enjoyed your time playing games; in fact, some of your most favorite memories might involve playing a game, like Monopoly, tag, or hide-and-seek.

Decide to chase a little of that happy feeling again as an adult—and use a game to do it.

It might be best to play a game with your child or another child you spend time with often, but it's not a requirement.

Pick the game you found most enjoyable as a kid and dig it out of the closet or find a way to play it online. Let yourself sink into the game and let go of all your adult worries.

Allow the game to distract you from the stress and pressure of being an adult and remind you what it's like to feel blissfully and effortlessly happy.

MAKE A DONATION

If you want to make a difference in the lives of others *and* get a boost of bliss, but you don't have a ton of free time, making a donation is a good way to do it.

Decide on a charity that is worthy of your money and donate!

Afterward, spend a moment or two imagining what your money will do for those it is meant to benefit. Maybe it will buy an underprivileged kid a coat for the winter, keep the local animal rescue stocked with kitty litter for another day, or feed a homeless person a holiday meal. Even if you didn't donate enough to cover a whole coat, all the litter boxes, or the whole meal, remind yourself that your donation contributed toward that outcome in a direct and meaningful way.

If you donated an item or items, think about the good they will do. Maybe your old blazer will help a survivor of domestic violence get a new job, or your gently used bike will make some kid's Christmas morning.

Let yourself feel proud of your good deed and enjoy the little slice of bliss you bought with your generosity.

FORGIVE YOURSELF FOR YOUR MISTAKES

We all make mistakes and sometimes hurt ourselves or those we're close to. We're human—it just happens! However, you may be one of the many people who find it relatively easy to forgive others but harder to forgive yourself.

In this exercise you'll practice forgiving yourself and open yourself up to a rush of relief and bliss as you do.

There's no need to think of any particular mistakes you have made for this one, since you're going to enact a sort of blanket forgiveness policy for all the mistakes, errors, and missteps you have made.

First, think about what it means to forgive; it means you are:

- Acknowledging that the offender did something that requires an apology (e.g., made a mistake, did something that hurt you, did something careless or thoughtless).
- Accepting the reality of the situation/accepting that it happened.
- Choosing to forgive the person for what they did.
- Actively working on putting it behind you.

Is there anything in that description that requires you to approve of the wrongdoing, celebrate it, or dismiss it entirely? No, of course not! When you forgive someone for hurting you, you are never under any obligation to erase the entire thing from your memory, tell them what they did was okay, or brush it off like nothing happened.

Now, apply this same forgiveness process to yourself. You don't need to approve of your mistake, celebrate it, or sweep it under the rug to forgive yourself for it. You just need to acknowledge that you made a mistake, accept that it happened, apologize to yourself—and perhaps apologize to anyone else who was affected by your mistake—and put it behind you.

Isn't it freeing to realize you have the power to forgive yourself and move on? Embrace that power and run with it!

FIND ONE POSITIVE STORY

There are so many positive, uplifting, and downright inspiring stories out there in the world. It might *seem* like the world is full of bad news, but that's really not the case. There are so many stories of good, kind, and wonderful things happening out there, just waiting for you to discover them.

To make a big deposit to your "bliss bank," take just a few minutes to search out a positive and uplifting story. You can leaf through the human-interest pieces in your local paper, watch the local news in the morning, search on popular news websites, or even check in with the local busybody and make a specific request for a positive and uplifting story.

These stories of joy, heroism, selflessness, or compassion will fill you with hope and happiness and a more positive outlook on the world. Whichever way you go about finding it, seeking out a positive story will not only give you more joy in the moment; it will also help get you accustomed to scanning information for the positive spin.

DO THE OPPOSITE

One of the most important things you can learn is that your not-so-blissful feelings do not control your destiny. For this exercise, you'll practice doing the opposite of what those negative or sad feelings would normally lead you to do.

1. **How do you feel right now?** Take a moment to recognize and identify it. Give it a name or label (e.g., "angry" or "wired").
2. **Now think about what you want to do.** How does this current feeling affect you and your desires? Note what it is you feel like doing.
3. **Decide what is the exact opposite of what you feel like doing.** If you feel like going home and hiding out in your room, go out to a crowded bar, restaurant, or other public place! If you feel like playing video games or watching TV, go for a run!

Doing the opposite will show you a possible future in which you are more in control and more full of bliss.

PICK ONE SKILL TO WORK ON

Whenever I get into "improvement mode," I want to work on improving everything all at once—but clearly, this can quickly get overwhelming. If you struggle with the same tendency, you might benefit from this exercise.

Think about all the skills or abilities you'd like to improve, then categorize them. The categories are up to you, but you might categorize them by urgency (*needs to improve immediately* to *nonurgent*), how much you value them (*extremely valuable* to *not very valuable*), or perhaps investment required (*tons of investment* to *not much investment*).

Consider which category you feel is most important in your life right now. Do you have the time to put in a ton of investment? Pick one from the *tons of investment* category. Are you ready to make a real, significant change? Pick one that is *extremely valuable*. Is there something that you want to change as fast as possible? Pick something that *needs to improve immediately*.

Simply picking one thing to focus on instead of dividing your attention among a dozen different enterprises can release a ton of stress, melt away tension, and give you a good dose of bliss.

TURN YOUR "SHOULDS" INTO "CANS"

Have you heard of "shoulding"? It's a behavior that saps your bliss and opens you up to unnecessary stress and self-defeat. To make sure you are open to bliss, try turning a "should" into a "can"!

First, identify some of your "shoulds." They are the implicit or explicit rules you have about how you *should* behave or how you *ought to* behave. We all have them, and they can be pretty sneaky.

Take a day to do this exercise prep if you need to: Carry around a journal and simply try to catch yourself "should"-ing throughout the day. When you do, write it down.

Now, the fun part—you get to turn those "shoulds" into "cans."

For every "should," think about what would be more exciting, bolder, or more positive, and write the appropriate "can" statement underneath it.

For example, if your "should" is "I should always be agreeable, even when other people aren't," your "can" might be "I can respond to people with authenticity, even if it means I'm not the most agreeable person."

Do this for every "should" and enjoy the blissful release of tension that comes with it!

SET SMART GOALS

When you have a good idea of how to reach out toward your dreams and you feel like anything is possible, it's much easier to find room for bliss in your mind and in your life. In order to achieve your dreams, you need to set SMART goals. SMART goals are not only "smart" goals to set; they also meet five criteria for effective goals.

To set some SMART goals for yourself, think about what you want to strive for. Do you have a big life goal? Perhaps a small, shorter-term goal instead? Whatever kind of vision you have for your future, pick one goal to run through the exercise with and get familiar with the process.

Next, frame your goal in the appropriate terms so that it is:

- **Specific:** your goal should be specific rather than vague (e.g., "Cut 1 minute off my mile" rather than "Run faster").
- **Measurable:** you should be able to measure your goal in a meaningful way (e.g., "Rate higher on the happiness measure my counselor gave me" rather than "Be happier").
- **Achievable:** your goal must be something you can actually, realistically achieve (e.g., "Raise $1,000 for the local food bank" rather than "End world hunger").
- **Relevant or Results-Focused:** your goal should be related to your desires and drives in life and focus on the endgame rather

than the process itself (e.g., "Lose 20 pounds" rather than "Work out fifty times").

- **Time-bound:** your goal must be accompanied by a deadline or "due date" by which you want to achieve it (e.g., "[Complete goal] by April 1, 2020" rather than "[Complete goal] ASAP").

Once you get the hang of it, it's easy enough to put your goals into SMART form. Putting in the effort will not only help you plan for future success; it will also help you feel more capable and competent, leading to a sense that true achievement is just around the corner.

Set SMART goals and embrace your bliss!

PRACTICE JOYFUL LIVING

The secret to bliss is not doing a couple of 5-minute exercises once in a while; it's practicing joyful living as a way of life. Joyful living is going through life with your eyes wide open to find the good, the positive, the awe-inspiring, and the uplifting all around you.

To open yourself up to experiencing bliss on a daily basis, give joyful living a test run. Here's what to do:

- Set aside a few minutes to practice, wherever you are and whatever is going on around you.
- Set an intention to find joy in anything that comes your way, no matter what it is.
- For those few minutes, practice finding joy in whatever happens. If the barista at a coffeehouse mispronounces your name, find joy in laughing about it. If you learn that your favorite lunch spot is closed for renovations, find joy in the opportunity to try a new cuisine.

Joy can be found just about everywhere, if you only open your eyes and look for it.

TRY ALTERNATE NOSTRIL BREATHING

This conscious breathing exercise is designed to get you feeling calm, collected, and blissful. If you have nostrils, you are a good candidate for it!

Here's how to do it:

1. Gently fold in your index and middle fingers on your right hand toward your palm, leaving your thumb, ring finger, and pinky finger extended.
2. Use your right thumb to gently hold your right nostril closed and breathe in slowly through your left nostril.
3. Use your right ring finger to hold your left nostril closed and release your right nostril.
4. Exhale through your right nostril.

That's it! Now, repeat this breathing exercise six times. Make sure to keep your right hand in the correct position (as described in step 1) and keep your breathing steady and regular. Don't speed it up or slow it down, and keep your inhales and exhales to a similar amount of time.

Practitioners of this method swear by its blissful effects, so keep an open mind and give it a try!

CHECK YOUR HAPPINESS GOALPOSTS

To give yourself the best chance at true happiness and bliss, it's important to pay attention to where your current goalposts for happiness are.

These goalposts might look something like this:

- I'll be happy when I get a girlfriend.
- I'll be happy when I graduate from college.
- I'll be happy when I get that promotion I want.
- I'll be happy when I finish that half-marathon.
- I'll be happy when my family learns to appreciate me.
- I'll be happy when I lose 30 pounds.

The truth is that none of these things will magically bring you happiness; happiness is a quality that comes from within yourself, not from external and arbitrary goalposts. Remind yourself that the best time to embrace happiness is right here and right now, no matter what goals you haven't quite reached yet.

The more you believe in this statement—a simple one, but still often difficult for us to accept—the more you will be able to experience bliss in the present.

CULTIVATE A HEALTHY RELATIONSHIP WITH MONEY

We know that money cannot buy happiness—after all, that's a pretty common concept in popular songs, movies, TV shows, and books. However, it's one thing to hear that and know it intellectually, and it's another thing to truly believe it.

To work on improving your relationship with money, go through this thought exercise:

1. Think about a celebrity or a personal acquaintance who would be described as rich but is not all that joyful. Ask yourself whether this contributes to the idea that money leads to happiness, or refutes it.
2. Consider someone you know or someone you've read or heard about who makes little to no money but is filled with joy and zest for life. Ask yourself whether this contributes to the idea that money leads to happiness, or refutes it.
3. Imagine that you had all the money you needed to live a fairly good life; would all your current problems go away?
4. Imagine that a mysterious billionaire showed up to offer you $10 billion in exchange for making a huge sacrifice, like giving up your partner, never speaking to your family again, losing your sense of taste, or never engaging in your favorite hobby again. Would you accept?

The point of this thought experiment (if you answer as most people would) is to show you that beyond having enough money to live at least a somewhat comfortable life, money truly cannot buy any more happiness.

If a billionaire can be miserable while a homeless person or someone living in poverty finds joy in everything, and if all your problems would not disappear with more money, and if you would refuse the mysterious billionaire and retain the love of your partner or family instead of taking the money, ask yourself what evidence there is for the theory that more money will make you more blissful.

If you're honest with yourself, you'll probably admit that there is little association between money and bliss. After a certain threshold (about $75,000 a year, last time the study was conducted), money simply doesn't make us any more joyful.

Remind yourself of this fact often, especially when you start to notice yourself obsessing about money. The more you repeat it to yourself, the more you'll believe it, and the better able you will be to find other ways to cultivate bliss!

PART 2

EXPERIENCE BLISS IN YOUR BODY

USE A FOAM ROLLER TO SQUEEZE OUT STRESS

It's a well-known fact that we store stress and tension in our muscles, and this problem offers you an excellent opportunity to heal yourself and find some bliss in your body.

Grab a foam roller in preparation for this exercise. Pro-tip: if you don't have a foam roller lying around the house, you can substitute a pool noodle for some of the moves!

Think about where you hold tension in your body. Is it in your back? Or maybe your shoulders? Some people hold their stress where they sit, in their buttocks and hips.

Wherever you find your stress, focus the foam roller there. For the purposes of explaining this exercise, we'll use the back as an example.

Start out by gently lying on the foam roller, but use your arms and legs to hold your body up and reduce the pressure on your muscles. Roll back and forth slowly, noticing where it feels best to release tension. Gradually introduce more pressure onto your muscles until it feels just a *tiny* bit uncomfortable.

As you feel the tension leave your muscles, feel it leaving your mind as well. Embrace this feeling and allow the stress to melt away, leaving room for bliss.

WASH YOUR HANDS—MINDFULLY

It doesn't always take a big momentous event to be happier, and this exercise is a prime example of that. Doing the familiar task of washing your hands in a slightly different way than you usually do it can actually help you feel happier and more positive.

After you use the bathroom, dirty your hands cooking, or before your next meal, take an extra minute or two to wash your hands.

Set your pace a bit slower than usual, but also be more thorough than usual. If you have particularly good-smelling soap, now is the time to use it!

Gently scrub every little bit of skin on your hands, paying special attention to underneath and around the nails. Notice the little details about your hands that you don't normally notice—the way the lines on your palms deepen when you close your hand, the way your nails change color from the bottom to the top, and the faint blue-green or purple of your veins just below the surface of your skin.

If it feels right, say a little prayer or a simple mantra about being grateful for your hands and what they allow you to do.

TOUCH YOUR TOES

A good stretch can do more than release tension in your muscles and improve your flexibility; it can also encourage you to be more mindful, more able to focus, and more blissful. To experience these benefits yourself, try this stretch:

1. Stand straight with your feet hip-distance apart, arms at your sides.
2. Inhale deeply through your nose. As you inhale, raise your arms up over your head, palms up, until they meet at the top.
3. Release your breath through your nose while you bend forward at the waist. Bend as far as you can without your back bowing or rounding. If you need to bend your knees to get a good stretch, go ahead and bend them.
4. Grasp your big toes with both hands (or hug your thighs or your calves close if you can't reach your toes) and hold this stretch for 10 seconds.
5. Release the stretch and stand up straight again, arms at your sides.
6. Repeat this stretch at least three times, or as many times as you feel like repeating it.

Thank yourself for the stretch and commit to carrying the sense of bliss and rejuvenation you feel with you throughout your day.

STRETCH TO THE SKY

All stretches have the benefits of improving flexibility and releasing tension, but stretching upward can also help you feel open-minded and open-hearted.

If you can, go outside for this quick stretch and follow these steps:

1. Stand straight with your feet hip-distance apart, arms at your sides.
2. Inhale through your nose while you raise your arms above your head, palms up. Let your palms meet right above your head and try to keep your arms straight.
3. Once your palms meet, turn them to the front and reach up as high as you can. You might get the urge to go up on the tips of your toes when you do this, and feel free to indulge that urge!
4. Hold the stretch for 10 seconds, breathing steadily in and out through your nose, then release the stretch and allow your arms to slowly fall back down to your sides, keeping your palms facing up until they reach your sides.
5. Take another deep breath in through your nose and out through your nose.
6. Repeat this stretch at least three times, or as many times as you feel like repeating it.

Remember to enjoy the stretch!

SHOW YOUR BODY SOME GRATITUDE

In today's world it's not always easy to feel blissful about our bodies. To ensure that you keep a positive perspective on your body and what it can do for you, make sure to show your body some gratitude once in a while.

If you need a little boost right now, give this exercise a try:

1. Stop whatever you're doing and grab a notebook or piece of paper and something to write with. If you keep a journal, this is a good idea for an entry.
2. Identify whatever action you were just engaged in (e.g., pushing your kids on the swing, exercising, washing the dishes, mowing the lawn, or even just typing at a keyboard).
3. Think about what abilities you needed to engage in that activity. For example, if you were pushing your kids on the swing, you would need to be using your leg muscles to stand, your spine to stay upright and stable, your arm and shoulder muscles to push and/or pull, your hands to grasp the chains or touch your child's back, your eyes to see where your child is, and on it goes.
4. Write down each of these things your body had to be able to do in order for you to participate in your last or current activity.
5. On paper and/or out loud, give your body some gratitude for each of these abilities. For example, you might write "Body, thank

you for allowing me to push my kids on the swing. Legs, thank you for holding me up so I can push them. Spine, thank you for staying stable and helping me be their rock. Arms and shoulders, thank you for giving me the strength I need to push them, challenge them, and hug them. Hands, thank you for allowing me to touch my children with love. Eyes, thank you for giving me the ability to enjoy their happy faces and guide their movements..."

Give your body gratitude for each of the amazing things it can do and bask in the bliss of being in sync with—and appreciative of—your body.

RUN LIKE THE WIND

As adults, we all too easily forget what running can feel like to a kid: exciting, revitalizing, and exhilarating. Many of us haven't run in years or perhaps even decades. Others might run once in a while on a treadmill, but they don't find joy in performing this regular healthy-living task.

To recapture this feeling, challenge yourself to a quick run. It doesn't have to be far, and you don't have to time yourself, but you should try to run as fast as you can.

Remember the phrase "run like the wind"? Or perhaps you've heard the old descriptor that someone was "running like the devil himself was chasing her"? That's how you should run.

Throw your adult concerns about how you will look and what people will think to the side. Make the decision to run with abandon, revel in the feelings that running brings, and try to run so fast that all your cares and concerns are left in the dust.

Treat your inner child to "running like the wind!"

LOOK IN THE MIRROR WITH LOVE

If you're like a lot of people, you don't always like what you see in the mirror. Or at least you don't like *everything* that you see in the mirror.

We all have some insecurities and areas where we wish we could make some changes, but we should always be mindful of appreciating ourselves overall. That's what this exercise can help you do.

Go to the closest and most convenient mirror. Your bathroom mirror is probably a good choice, but any old mirror will do.

1. **First, take a minute to simply look at yourself in the mirror.** Don't make any particular expressions yet; just take a good, long look at your face. Get to know it in a way that you haven't before.
2. **Next, try saying a few positive affirmations to yourself.** Make them healing thoughts that will help build your self-esteem and self-confidence. No negative talk allowed!
3. **Now, give yourself a grin—a big, natural smile at yourself in the mirror.** If you have trouble putting on a natural smile, think about one of your happiest memories and try to relive that feeling.
4. **Note any laugh lines or smile wrinkles, the brightness in your eyes, the glow of your face, or anything else that acts as a visible reminder of your happiness** and appreciate them for what they represent—a life filled with laughter!

EAT A HEALTHY SNACK

This simple and satisfying exercise will make you feel good *and* encourage you to be healthier—it's a win-win!

To get a quick boost of bliss in your body, look in your fridge and find something healthy, quick, and easy. An apple is a good choice, or maybe a handful of almonds, a yogurt with some granola, or some carrots with hummus.

Whatever your choice of healthy snack, don't just gobble it up! Find a place to sit down and limit the distractions around you. Turn off your TV, turn off your phone, and put away your to-do list—whether it's physical or mental.

Take small, mindful bites of your snack. With each bite, remind yourself that you are doing something good for yourself. Think about how every bit of your healthy snack will help create energy you can use to engage in your favorite hobby, play with your children, or work toward a better, happier, and healthier you.

Give yourself a pat on the back for doing something that is good for both your mind and your body, and remember that feeling as you continue with your day.

GIVE YOURSELF A MINI MASSAGE

It might not be as luxurious and relaxing as getting a massage from a professional, but getting a mini massage can have some wonderful benefits, even if you're the one doing the work!

To get a little of that pampered feeling without the pampered price tag, sit up straight in a chair or on the edge of your bed. Take a deep breath in through your nose. As you exhale, place your hands on the tops of your shoulders, palms down, fingers pointing behind you.

Breathe deeply and regularly as you gently squeeze your shoulders. Move from the tops of your shoulders to the sides of your neck, the back of your neck, and your shoulder blades—if you can reach them!

Next, cross your arms across your chest and give each of your arms a squeeze with the other hand. Rub your upper arms and lower arms in the same way.

Finally, finish your mini massage with a quick massage of each hand, focusing on the center of the palm. Take a deep breath through your nose and slowly, gently exhale through your nose to end the relaxing experience.

DO A BODY SCAN

A body scan can help you pinpoint areas where you are holding on to tension, relax any muscles that need relaxing, and get in touch with your body. Strengthening the connection between your mind and your body is an excellent way to feel more blissful, grounded, and happy.

Lie down on your bed, a yoga mat, or the floor (preferably a clean floor!) with your arms at your sides and your legs straight, feet hip-distance apart. Close your eyes and begin to pay attention to your breath as it gradually fills your lungs and slowly leaves your body.

Once you feel that your mind is quiet and ready to begin, think about your toes. Think about how they feel, whether you have any tension, itches, ticklish sensations, or any other sensations. Notice how they feel in your shoes or in the open air. Make a conscious effort to release any tension in your toes.

When your toes feel relaxed, move on to your feet. Engage in the same process of observing, noticing, and relaxing. After you repeat this process with your feet, continue on to your ankles, your calves, your thighs, and so on.

When you finish the process on your neck, move to your face. You hold a lot of tension and worry in your face, so it's important to spend some time working on relaxing your muscles, letting go of the worry lines in your forehead, and allowing your eyebrows to rest in their natural, default position. You probably won't notice how much tension there is in your facial muscles until you make a conscious effort to relax them, but you'll definitely feel a difference afterward!

After relaxing your face, move on to your head. Think about how your head *feels*, what thoughts are bouncing around causing trouble, and whether you have any aches or pain anywhere in your head. Let all of this muscle tension go.

Take a deep breath through your nose. As you exhale, visualize all the negative thoughts, worries, tension, and pain leaving your body with your breath. Take as many breaths as you need to feel like you have emptied out all the unwanted thoughts and feelings, then finish with one final deep breath.

Open your eyes, get up, and go on with your day in a more peaceful, blissful state of mind (and body)!

EXFOLIATE YOUR SKIN

Doing just one simple thing for your body can be surprisingly relaxing and bliss-inducing. There are many such things you can do for your body, but one good idea is to exfoliate your skin.

When you exfoliate, you not only shed the dead skin cells that have been lying on top of your healthy skin; you offer yourself an opportunity to shed any negative thoughts and feelings—aka clutter—and replace them with bliss.

Grab a loofah or some exfoliating gloves and decide what parts of your body need a good scrub. If you have time for a shower, a full-body exfoliation is a great choice. If not, consider exfoliating just your face, your hands and arms, or your legs and feet.

As you prepare to exfoliate, think about shedding the negative or simply unnecessary thoughts and feelings to make room for more bliss-ful ones. Visualize bringing the clutter to the surface of your skin and see it being scrubbed away in your mind's eye.

Feel how wonderful it is to be clean, smooth, and fresh—both inside and out—and now that you've decluttered, find ways to fill in the extra space inside with joy.

DO A SILLY DANCE

One excellent method for feeling more joyful is to exercise your creativity. Remember how you could always entertain yourself as a child, even if you had nothing but your own body to entertain yourself with? Like most children, you probably moved around a lot. This exercise will tap into that natural urge to move and express yourself through that movement.

If you need a boost of creativity and joy, come up with a new and unique dance. It doesn't have to be in public, and it doesn't need to be a good, choreographed dance; it just needs to be a dance that is authentically "you."

Think about what joy and creativity feel like to you and use your body to act out those feelings. Throw your hands in the air, jump, kick your feet, tap out a rhythm, clap, or do anything else that helps you engage in a unique, meaningful, and authentic dance that accurately captures your joyful self.

We tend to stop engaging in creative practices like doing silly dances as we grow older, but there's no reason we have to stop altogether! Feed both your inner artist and inner child at once with this exercise.

GIVE YOURSELF A HUG

Sometimes all you need to feel a little bit better is a hug! If no one is around to solicit a hug from, try giving yourself a hug.

Sit or stand straight with your arms relaxed at your sides. Breathe deeply and try to fill your heart and your mind with a sense of love and compassion. Bring your arms up in front of your chest and wrap them around yourself as you exhale.

Stay in this position for a few minutes as you breathe slowly and regularly. When you inhale, expand your chest and cultivate that love and compassion. When you exhale, squeeze your arms a bit tighter around yourself and extend that love and compassion to yourself. Continue for a few minutes, or until you feel noticeably lighter and happier.

You might feel silly giving yourself a hug, so you might want to try this one in a private place. But if it works, who cares how you look doing it?

TRY FULL-BODY RELAXATION

If you're feeling tension, stress, and aches throughout your body, there's nothing like a quick full-body relaxation practice to get you feeling happier, healthier, and more blissful!

If you want to work on getting more grounded and connected to your body, the "Do a Body Scan" exercise earlier in this part might be a better option for you; however, if you just want some pure and simple relaxation, this is the exercise for you.

Start out by dimming the lights in the room you want to practice your relaxation in. Your bedroom is a good option, as you have your bed as a natural resting space—just don't get too comfortable, since you don't want to fall asleep! A couch, yoga mat, or even a towel can work just fine too.

Lie down on your back with your arms and legs resting wherever you find them most comfortable. If your lower back grumbles about lying flat, roll up some towels or grab a foam roller to place beneath your knees. This will take the pressure off your lower back and let you focus on truly relaxing.

Begin with a deep inhale through your nose. When you've reached the top of your inhale, pause for a moment and focus on one area of your body that is holding tension. Pause again, and exhale all your breath through your mouth while concentrating all your relaxation intentions on that area of your body. When your lungs are completely empty, pause for another short moment, then start over. Continue until you have sent relaxing sensations to every inch of your body.

When you run out of areas to focus on, continue breathing with this method and visualize big waves of calming, soothing energy washing over your entire body, beginning at the top of your head and gently flowing all the way down to your toes. Imagine this wave pushing out all of your aches and pains, all of your tension, and all of your worries. Open yourself up to the bliss and embrace the opportunity!

FILL YOUR LUNGS—ALL THE WAY

When you take a deep breath, you might think you fill your lungs all the way; however, the truth is that there is usually a little bit of space left. This exercise will help you learn how to play with this space and use it to bring yourself more peace, enhance your bliss, and revitalize your mental state.

Begin with a deep inhale through your nose. When you've reached the top of your inhale, pause for a moment, then take in just a bit more air. Pause again, and exhale all of your breath through your mouth. Pause for a moment when your lungs are empty and start again.

When you first try this exercise, use this routine: 5 seconds in, 1 second pause, top off, 1 second pause, 5 seconds out, 1 second pause.

In other words, inhale deeply for 5 seconds, pause for 1 second, take in a bit more, pause for another second, exhale for 5 seconds, then pause for another second once your lungs are empty.

Continue breathing this way for at least five repetitions. As you practice this exercise more often, challenge yourself to increase the pauses to 2 seconds each, then 3 seconds each.

GET FRESH AND CLEAN

Sometimes the best way to boost your mood is to get clean! Even if you're not particularly sweaty, dusty, or dirty, a shower or bath just hits the spot.

To take advantage of the mood benefits a quick bath or shower can provide, simply set the temperature to your own customized sweet spot and hop in.

As you clean your external self, take a few moments to simply enjoy the feeling of getting clean. Think about how good it feels to clean yourself off after a long, sweaty, tiring day and extend this sense of cleansing to your mind. Allow it to wipe away the busyness and grime of your day.

When you step out and start to dry off, thank yourself for taking this opportunity to do some internal and external maintenance. Commit to pairing your internal and external maintenance more often and scrubbing your inside along with your outside. Show yourself some appreciation and enjoy the feeling of being squeaky clean!

STRETCH LIKE A CAT/COW

If you've ever tried yoga, you might be familiar with the poses nicknamed "Cat" and "Cow." These poses are intended as part of a breathing exercise, alternating between them as you inhale and exhale.

To try these stretches, get down on all fours. A yoga mat or other soft padding might help your knees if the floor is hard. Start with a straight back, head facing straight down toward the ground.

Begin with a deep inhale through your nose. As you inhale, arch your back like a cat and pull your belly button up toward your spine. Roll in as far as you can, until your head is facing your pelvis.

Hold this stretch for a moment, then exhale through your nose. As you exhale, move back down to a neutral spine, then roll into a curved spine. Drop your belly button toward the ground while keeping your hips and shoulders in roughly the same spots as before. At the same time, lift your head up to look at the sky.

Alternate between the Cat and Cow poses for at least five breaths and enjoy the sense of peace and calm the stretch brings!

INDULGE IN SOMETHING DELICIOUS

It's important to feed your body the fuel it needs, and the fuel it needs is healthy food; however, it's also important to treat yourself at least once in a while!

Instead of choosing a snack based on its caloric content, its carbohydrate count, or the grams of sugar it contains, choose a snack based on nothing but how it tastes. Pick something you really enjoy and rarely let yourself eat.

Some delicious suggestions include:

- A cupcake
- A candy bar
- An order of hot, salty french fries
- A piece of cake
- A scoop (or two) of ice cream
- A small bag of crispy, kettle-cooked chips

As you eat your snack, keep your mind on how you feel. Savor the taste of your snack and savor the feeling of treating yourself to something delicious. Thank your body for your ability to taste and enjoy food.

Try to indulge in these kinds of treats only once every couple of weeks. This will not only help you stay healthier; it will also keep the experience feeling rare and special.

MEDITATE IN A NEW PLACE OR POSITION

If you've ever gone out of your way to try something new, you know what a positive impact it can have on your happiness! Add something new to something tried-and-true, like meditating, to maximize your bliss.

The most popular way to meditate is by sitting on a cushion on the ground with your legs drawn up into a "crisscross" position. This is a popular way to meditate because it's comfortable and easy, but adding variety to your routine can enhance all of meditation's many benefits. If you typically meditate in the previously described place and position, give one of these options a try. If you really don't like it, you're under no obligation to keep practicing it. But who knows, you may find that you have a new favorite practice!

- Sitting on a straight-backed chair with your feet on the floor.
- Lying on a yoga mat or other semi-cushy surface.
- Standing outside in a quiet, secluded spot.
- Sitting with your back against a tree and your knees drawn up to your chest.

If you want to take your mood up a notch, give meditating in a new place or in a new position a try.

HAVE A BALL

We all know that exercise is good for us, but it's still hard to get ourselves moving sometimes. If you have trouble motivating yourself, give this quick exercise a try.

If you have a favorite sport, you probably have that sport's ball (e.g., baseball, basketball, soccer ball) lying around the house somewhere. If not, you might have to get creative; do you have a beach ball? An exercise ball? If all else fails, a balloon?

Whatever type of ball you can get your hands on will work. All you have to do is play!

On one hand, this exercise may be one of the easiest and simplest exercises in this book; on the other hand, you may be one of the many adults who think, "How do I just 'play'?" We lose some of our imagination and creativity as we get older, but it's not necessarily gone for good.

Take your ball and find some way to play with it. Toss it in the air and catch it, kick it around, or swat it around the room like a curious cat. Spend 5 minutes playing with your ball and enjoy the extra spontaneity, playfulness, and vitality that come along with it.

PRACTICE 5-MINUTE YOGA

If you've never tried yoga before, this exercise is a great way to start. Yoga has tons of benefits for the regular practitioner, and just about anyone can do it.

To do a mini yoga practice in 5 minutes or less, follow these steps:

For the seated portion:

1. Sit on the floor—on a cushion or yoga mat if you have one—with your legs crossed and your hands loosely resting on your knees or thighs.
2. Start with deep, regular breathing, both in and out through your nose.
3. Bring your hands to the center of your chest (i.e., at "heart center"), palms together and fingers pointing up. Set an intention for your yoga session and for the rest of the day, like "I will be fully present."
4. Place your right hand on your left knee and turn your head to the left, twisting a bit. Do the same movement on the other side, then repeat twice on each side.
5. Put your hands out in front of you, fingers laced together, and round your back as you stretch them forward.
6. Put your hands behind your back, fingers again laced together, and arch your back as you push your interlaced fingers back behind you.
7. Repeat the last two back stretches two more times.

For the standing portion:

1. Stand up with your feet hip-distance apart, hands at your sides, and bring your hands up over your head to meet, palms facing one another, as you breathe in deeply through your nose.
2. Breathe out through your nose as you bend forward at the waist, keeping your back straight. Try to touch your toes. If you can't, keep your back straight and bend your knees a bit to help you reach them. Hold for several seconds.
3. Breathe in through your nose and lift your back halfway up, so your back is parallel to the floor—and still straight! You can rest your hands lightly on your thighs, calves, or wherever else they feel comfortable.
4. Breathe out and fold forward again for a full, touch-your-toes stretch.
5. Breathe in and stand up, bringing your hands all the way up and around to meet over your head again.
6. Breathe out and bring your palms down to your heart center. Repeat the standing portion four more times.

Finish this exercise, and you'll notice that even 5 minutes of yoga can be a significant mood-enhancer!

TAKE THE TIME TO ENJOY
A LUXURIOUS BATH

There's nothing that can feel quite as sumptuous, lavish, and self-pampering as taking a long, relaxing bath. If you've never really been a bath person, this is an excellent time to start!

This exercise can be tacked on to the end of a routine bath or used as a quick reset and refresh at the end of a hectic day. Even a short bath can have a profound impact on your mood.

- Get started by setting a warm, comfortable temperature and filling the bath. Don't make it too hot—you want to feel warm and cozy, not like you're boiling!
- Turn off your phone and lock your bathroom door.
- Clear out any clutter from the bathroom, and put your supplies (shampoo, conditioner, bath salts, maybe even a cup of tea!) within easy reach.
- To feel particularly pampered, light some candles and put on some soft and soothing music.
- Sprinkle the bath with some moisturizing oil, natural extracts, or bath salts. Use additives that enhance the experience of the bath, through making your skin feel extra smooth and soft, releasing a pleasant fragrance, or both.

- Breathe slowly and completely, focusing on the clam and the gentle feel of the water.

As you sink into the bath, let your state of mind match your physical state—give in to the relaxation and bliss of the moment.

MAKE YOURSELF A DRINK

Is there anything as satisfying as a well-deserved, handcrafted drink at the end of a long, hard day? If there is, I want to hear about it! A home-made favorite cocktail or special tea can get you into a more blissful state of mind almost immediately.

To turn a simple drink into a bliss-enhancing exercise, just keep these three suggestions in mind:

- Instead of hurriedly making your favorite libation or ordering it from a waiter or bartender, make it yourself—mindfully. Stay focused on the task at hand and dedicate yourself to doing it well and with your full attention.
- Don't do anything else while you drink it. Just sit and experience your drink with no distractions. Leave the TV off and your phone in your pocket or purse and simply be for a few minutes.
- With each sip, remind yourself to savor the taste and the smell! Really taste the flavor, swirl it around in your mouth, and breathe in the aroma before you drink.

Remember, the drink doesn't need to be an alcoholic one! Make any drink a rare or special treat.

PAMPER YOURSELF

This is a really open-ended activity, which makes it perfectly suited to customization.

A fabulous way to inject your day with a bit more bliss is to make yourself *feel* fabulous! This might be something completely different for you, but here are some common activities that many people find help them feel pampered and fabulous:

- Getting a long massage or a facial.
- Buying a new book you've been wanting to read.
- Buying yourself something really delicious for dinner.
- Splurging on a new piece of clothing or another item you've had your eye on.
- Getting a manicure and pedicure (and yes, many men can and do enjoy manicures and pedicures as well!).
- Treating yourself to a fancy coffee or a sweet treat you rarely indulge in.
- Going to see a guilty pleasure movie.

Whatever it is that makes you feel pampered, fabulous, and luxurious—do it! You shouldn't pamper yourself all the time, but make sure you do it at least once in a while to invite more bliss into your life.

CHALLENGE YOURSELF TO A PHYSICAL TASK

Rest, relaxation, and comfort are all vital parts of our self-care. No matter how much we might like to have boundless energy and stay on the go all the time, humans simply weren't made for that level of activity.

However, we weren't made for *all* rest and relaxation either! It's extremely important that we stay physically active, both to our physical health and to our mental health. One way to get a bit more active and boost your well-being at the same time is to challenge yourself to some sort of physical task.

When you engage in a little competition, even if it's only competition with yourself, you often enjoy a burst of energy and motivation as well as a sense of satisfaction once you've finished.

To harness this revitalization, challenge yourself to a task that involves physical activity. It can be customized based on your health and activity level, and it could be anything from 5 minutes of sustained speed-walking to 5 minutes of pull-ups! The challenge itself doesn't need to meet any certain specifications, other than that it is truly challenging for you.

Are you up to your own challenge? Give it a shot!

STRIKE A POSE

If you haven't already heard the news, there's some recent evidence that simply striking certain poses can make you feel more self-confident, more self-assured, and happier. If you need a little boost to your self-esteem *and* your mood, give one of these poses a try:

- **The Superman:** stand with your hands folded into fists on your hips, knuckles facing in, and elbows out wide. If you want to feel capable, competent, and content with yourself, this pose is the one for you.
- **V for Victory:** stand tall with your arms spread in a wide "V" shape above your head. This pose can make you feel like you just won a serious competition!
- **The VIP:** sit with your feet up on a desk or table, crossed at the ankles, and your hands folded behind your head. This will make you feel smooth, confident, and in control.
- **Top Dog:** stand at a desk or table and place both palms on it, fingers pointing slightly outward, and lean over the desk. This pose can make you feel large and in charge.
- **Thankful:** stand with your arms raised to shoulder height and your hands straight out to the sides, palms facing up, then tilt your head back a bit to look up at the sky or ceiling. This simple

pose will make you feel more open-minded, open-hearted, and open to bliss in your life.

- **The Heart Center:** sit cross-legged or stand with your feet a fist's width apart and place your palms together, facing one another, in front of your chest. This is called the heart center in yoga, and it will help you to feel more calm, joyful, and connected with your authentic self.

If you try all of these poses and find that none of them work for you, feel free to come up with your own! It doesn't really matter what the pose is, as long as it makes you feel happier, more joyful, or more blissful.

TENSE AND RELAX

If you're having a hard time relaxing just by "trying" to relax, this exercise may help you find an alternate route to tranquility in your body.

Find a quiet, comfortable, and private space. Dim the lights and turn off anything that might disrupt you. If you need some white noise to relax, try turning on a sound machine at a low level.

Lie on your bed or on a carpeted floor and let your arms and legs rest wherever is comfortable. Close your eyes and begin breathing slowly and regularly. Starting with your toes, follow these steps:

1. Direct your attention to your toes. Notice how they feel and whether there is any tension in them.
2. Squeeze and flex your toes as hard as you can (without hurting yourself) and hold the squeeze for 3 seconds.
3. Release your toes and allow all the tension to run out of them.

Once you finish relaxing your toes, move on to your feet, then your ankles, and so on until you reach your head. If you find that holding the squeeze for 3 seconds didn't release all the tension, try holding for another 3 seconds.

BREATHE WITH YOUR DIAPHRAGM

Breathing exercises are great ways to invite some more bliss into your body and your mind. They help you get calm and centered and can open you up to the joy all around you; however, it's important to practice these breathing exercises correctly.

One such way to make sure you are practicing effective breathing techniques is to get comfortable and familiar with the feeling of breathing in and out with your diaphragm.

To get in some practice, follow these guidelines:

1. Lie back with your knees slightly bent and your head supported. Place one hand on your chest and the other just below your ribs.
2. Inhale through your nose in a slow, smooth rhythm that causes your stomach to press against your hand.
3. Purse your lips, tense your stomach, and draw your muscles toward your spine as you exhale.
4. Repeat steps 2 and 3 with the hand on your chest remaining as still as possible.

The point of these breathing exercises is to allow your diaphragm to work as intended, strengthening it and helping you to breathe more efficiently.

PRACTICE MORNING MINDFULNESS IN YOUR BODY

Mindfulness is never a bad idea—it can help with so many things, including clearing your head after a long day, reenergizing after a slump, and giving you a chance to check in with yourself throughout the day. It can also be used to enhance your bliss and start you off on the right foot in the morning.

Here's what to do:

1. As soon as you wake up, remind yourself of your commitment to your practice. You can use an alarm, a sticky note, a string tied around your finger, or anything else that will help you remember.
2. Keep your breath regular and even as you begin to focus your awareness on your body.
3. Take a few deep breaths as you direct your attention toward identifying and recognizing any sensations you are feeling in your body.
4. Once you have a good handle on how you're feeling, engage in a mindful stretch. Stretch in whatever way feels good, but try to extend the stretch to your entire body. Notice how good it feels to get that first morning stretch in.

End your session with gratitude for yourself and enjoy the post-morning mindfulness bliss!

TAKE A BRISK WALK

Slow, mindful strolls are a great way to enhance your sense of calm, but there's something to be said for brisk walks as well. They can get your blood pumping, clear your head, and give you an extra dose of motivation.

To get a boost of energy along with your boost in mood, try taking a brisk, fast-paced walk instead of a more measured walk. Challenge yourself to walk just a bit faster than is comfortable for you. You shouldn't be sweating and panting, but you should find it difficult to carry on a normal conversation.

As you walk, notice the scenery around you. Take note of anything interesting, pretty, or otherwise pleasing to look at. Keep a running list of all these things you notice in your head.

From beginning to end, take deep breaths in through your nose and exhale them through your mouth. This will help you get energized and make sure you're getting the oxygen you need to keep pace.

Once you reach your destination, think back over your mental list and let the thought of these pretty, interesting, and pleasant things make you smile.

CREATE GOOD-VIBE WAVES

In this exercise, you'll create some "good-vibe" waves or "feel-good" waves and send them all throughout your body, bringing bliss to every inch of you.

Find a quiet and comfortable place to lie down and follow these steps:

1. Lie comfortably and close your eyes, gently holding them shut (rather than squeezing them shut).
2. Take a few moments to gather up some good thoughts. Think about all the good things in your life and in the world right now. Pull all the goodness and beauty and inspiration from these things and form them into a ball in your mind.
3. Imagine this ball at your heart center—the center of your chest, near your heart. Visualize it growing bigger and bigger as you add more positivity to it. If you need some more material, add in some love and kindness from your most cherished relationships, some inspiration and elevation from your favorite motivational speakers or religious leaders, and the compassion and heart-warming sensations you get when you hear about people doing the right thing when faced with some tempting alternatives.
4. Focus on the sensation of holding the ball: it's soft, smooth, and squishy—sort of like a stress ball. Hold on to this ball firmly but

lightly and feel it begin to pulse in your hands. Feel the gentle movement that warms your hands with each pulse.

5. As you visualize this ball pulsing, see it sending out shock waves of goodness with each pulse. These waves roll all the way through your body, to the top of your head, the tips of your toes, and the ends of your fingers.

6. Feel all this goodness as it travels through you and allow it to infuse your body with bliss and good vibes. Really focus on how it feels to send these good vibes through your leg muscles, your arm muscles, and your whole body.

7. Spend a few minutes sending waves from your heart center, then imagine taking the ball and putting it away, back into your mind, safely stored for future good vibes.

8. Get up and get on with your day, but make sure to take the good vibes with you!

TAKE A QUICK SPIN ON A BIKE

Getting outdoors, taking in some good views, and breathing in a little fresh air can do wonders for your mood as well as your body. Taking a bike ride is one of the best ways to do this, especially if you're not a fitness enthusiast or if you're nervous about taking a long walk by yourself.

To give this exercise a try, simply hop on your bike and pedal off in a direction with something interesting ahead!

As you ride, focus on keeping your lungs open and your mind clear. Allow the beauty and peace of nature or the energizing rhythm of city life to fill your head and heart with happiness.

If you don't have a bike, you can substitute a stationary bike, whether you have one at home or you have to take a quick trip to the nearby gym. You won't get the nature and fresh air or revitalizing city ride aspects, but you can use it as an opportunity to practice visualization!

SIGN UP FOR A FITNESS CLASS

One of the best ways you can boost your bliss is by ensuring that your health is in tip-top shape—or at least somewhat good shape! It's much easier for you to feel happy, healthy, and blissful when your body is also happy and healthy.

Go online with your laptop or smartphone and search for fitness classes near you. There are bound to be at least a few! Think about what sounds most interesting to you or most appropriate for your fitness level. If your heart is in good shape and you like dance music, a Zumba class might be a good choice for you. If you're just getting started with exercise, then a gentle yoga or water aerobics class are both great options.

Sign up for at least one class. You don't need to get an annual pass or buy a ten-pack of classes; just buy one and see how you feel after your class.

After you've signed up, give yourself a pat on the back for doing something good for yourself and commit to following through on it.

PUT YOUR TOES IN THE SAND

There's nothing quite like the beach: the sound of waves crashing, the smell of ocean in the air, the breeze that brings you some of that salty sea spray. Just picturing it can make you feel calm and blissful!

Put the magic of the beach to work for you by finding a little bit of sand. If you're near a beach, that's clearly the best place to find some sand for this exercise. If not, see if you can find a bit of sand somewhere else—a sandbox at a playground, the sandpit at the local park, or even some vaguely sand-like dirt outside your house!

Follow these steps to get some beachy bliss:

1. Take your shoes and socks off, if you're wearing any.
2. Sit or stand with your feet in the sand. Direct your attention to the sensations in your feet; wiggle your toes and rock back and forth on the balls of your feet.
3. Close your eyes and visualize the beach. See the sand and the water, smell the salty air, and hear the waves rolling in and out.

Stay here for a few minutes and soak in the bliss of a (virtual) beach day!

TOUCH SOMETHING WITH AN INTERESTING TEXTURE

Our minds and our bodies are even more connected than we might think. Even small movements and actions can have a big impact on our thought process and our mood.

If you want to pull yourself out of your head and into the present and find some joy in a small thing at the same time, try simply touching something!

Look around you and find an object that looks like it has an interesting texture or pleasant feel to it. You might pick a fun fabric, like velvet, satin, or something embroidered. You could also find an artistic decor piece that is slippery smooth, lumpy and bumpy, or has a rough, sandpapery surface. Take a peek and you're sure to find something that will feel interesting.

Take a few moments to simply feel the object. Pick it up (if it's small enough to pick up), or just sit beside it and explore it with your fingertips.

Focus on the sensations you are experiencing and simply enjoy the feeling of something new and interesting.

GET TWISTY

One of yoga's best contributions to body bliss is the twisting it incorporates. Twists are movements we don't naturally engage in very often, meaning that just a little twist can make a big difference in how we feel!

To get your mood-boosting, heart-opening, body-pleasing twists on, try these steps:

1. Lie flat on your back with your arms at your sides and your feet hip-width apart.
2. Bring one knee up to your chest (or as close as you can comfortably get it to your chest) and, using your opposite hand, gently guide it to the other side of your body.
3. Keep your back flat and your shoulder blades pressed into the ground as you twist.
4. For an extra stretch, turn your head to the opposite side (e.g., if you bring your right leg up, use your left hand to guide it to the left side of your body and turn your head right).
5. Hold for at least 30 seconds or a full 2 minutes, then repeat on the other side.

If that isn't enough of a twist for you, here's another twist that can bring you bliss—along with some sweat!

1. Standing with your feet together or a fist's width apart, keep your back straight while you bend your knees like you're about to sit in a chair. Keep your shoulders upright and your face forward!
2. Put your palms together in front of your chest, fingers pointing up, and lean forward until your elbows are just above your knees.
3. Next, use your elbow as leverage to twist your upper body to one side while your lower body remains in place (e.g., keeping your hands at the center of your chest, place your left elbow outside your right knee and use it to twist to the right).
4. Hold the twist for at least a few moments, or even a full minute or two, then repeat on the other side.

Make sure to keep your knees and hips even—you should twist only from the waist up.

Don't worry if you find this twist difficult. It's supposed to be difficult! Keep practicing whenever you get a chance and you'll find that your flexibility and your mood will improve.

SQUEEZE A STRESS BALL

If you've ever squeezed a stress ball before, you know that it can be immensely satisfying! There's something about the squishy, rubbery feeling complemented by the slight resistance that strips away your stress, clears your mind, and helps you feel happier.

If you're not sure what the fuss is all about when it comes to stress balls, try these "exercises" and see for yourself:

- **Simply squeeze!** Tighten your hand around the ball until you feel real resistance.
- **Roll the ball in your hand.** This will help you improve your dexterity and facilitate problem-solving.
- **Toss the ball from one hand to the other.** Not only will you practice your fine motor skills, but you will also get a boost in brainstorming and idea generation.
- **Hold the ball between two fingers at a time, squeezing slightly.** This will give your fingers a rare workout and help you clear your mind, leaving more room for bliss.

Something as simple as a squishy rubber ball can have a surprising impact on your state of mind and help you to find your bliss.

PLAY WITH SOME PLAYDOUGH

Here's another way to enhance your bliss by engaging your inner child: play with playdough!

Do you remember how fun it was in elementary school when they broke out the playdough? In my classroom, it was like Christmas had come early!

To make your inner child smile, pick up some playdough from the store (or, if you're feeling super artistic or industrious, you can search for a recipe online and create your own). Take a minute to just play with it and enjoy the feeling of the playdough in your hands.

Next, come up with some sort of design or mini sculpture you'd like to make. The sky is the limit! Be creative and don't confine yourself to making something "realistic."

Playing with this squishy, moldable substance is a great way for children to boost their hand-eye coordination, improve dexterity, and prepare their hands for those fine motor skills they will soon be learning in school. Luckily, it also has some great benefits for adults—it can boost your creative thinking, keep fidgety hands busy, and help you clear your head and find some extra joy!

PLAY TAG

You probably already know that exercise and physical activity are some of the best ways to boost your bliss and find joy in your body. However, it can be tough to motivate yourself to exercise, especially when you don't really enjoy it. One effective way to boost your motivation is to basically trick yourself into exercising through a fun activity or game.

Playing tag is a great option for sneaking some bliss-boosting physical activity into your day and delighting your inner child at the same time.

Find someone to play with who's on board with a game of tag. This will probably be your child, niece or nephew, grandchild, or another child whom you regularly spend time with, but don't assume there are no adults who would be happy to join in! To make it more challenging (and more fun), play somewhere with obstacles and places to hide.

As you play, allow that smile to shine and the giggles and the triumphant cries of "Got you!" to bring you joy.

GET HYDRATED

We feel the most bliss in our bodies when we take good care of our bodies. A simple but vital way to take good care of your body is to make sure you are hydrated. It also gives you an opportunity to enjoy the heavenly feeling of quenching your thirst with clear, cool water—a blissful feeling if there ever was one!

If you feel tired, drained, a little moody, or hungry even after eating, give hydration a try. It's a pretty simple two-step process:

1. Pour yourself a full glass of water and drink it!
2. Repeat until you are no longer thirsty or you feel like your belly will slosh around with every step.

It can be easy to forget to hydrate with everything else going on in our busy lives, but the benefits justify putting in a little extra effort to keep hydration in mind.

After you've hydrated, take a moment to think about how you feel now. Do you feel a little less tired, drained, moody, or hungry? Don't be surprised if some of your bad mood or fatigue melted away! Keep that in mind next time you find yourself in need of some mood boosting.

DO A CARTWHEEL

When was the last time you did a cartwheel? I'm guessing it was a long time ago!

It's common to stop doing fun and silly active things like cartwheels as you age, but it's not a requirement! Doing something physical—especially if it's fun and silly—can give you a sense of accomplishment and exhilaration and remind you how to find joy in your body.

In case you've forgotten how to do a cartwheel, here's how:

1. Clear a path of at least 10 feet or so in front of you.
2. Put your hands above your head and take a quick step forward with your dominant foot.
3. Push off with your feet and forward with your arms, tilting sideways as you go. Bring your hands down to the ground and hold your wrists steady but not too firm—you don't want to sprain a wrist!
4. Let your momentum swing your feet up and over your head, all the way to the other side.
5. Keep your hands up for balance and stand tall and proud once you've come to a stop, then thank your body for all the amazing things it can do!

DECIDE ON YOUR FAVORITE FEATURES

We often hear about the features that people *don't* like about themselves, but that doesn't contribute to bliss. What *does* contribute to bliss is thinking about your favorite features instead of your least favorite features. You don't have to have a perfect body to appreciate it!

When you have a few minutes, grab a pen and paper and start thinking about what you like about your body. Come up with at least three features that you find appealing.

The feature could be an area or muscle group, like your toned calves or strong back. It could also be something tiny, like your eyelashes or your fingernails. Some common favorites are facial features, like your eyes, your lips, or your nose.

Whatever it is, write down a short sentence stating that you like this feature or part of your body.

The more often you do this exercise, the more you will come to value your body and appreciate your best features.

Commit to finding joy and pride in your body instead of dwelling on supposed flaws, and both your mind and body will thank you.

PRACTICE PERFECT POSTURE

It's not only what you do with your body during exercise and rest that has a big impact on your mood and health; it's what you do with it all the time that matters! Even when you're not actively working out, stretching, or drifting off to sleep, how you hold yourself can make quite a difference.

If you want to invite a bit more bliss into your life and your body, pay attention to your body and practice good posture. Here are some things to check in on:

- **Are you slumped over?** It's hard on your back when you have an unnatural curve or hump in your spine! Focus on sitting up straight. If it helps, pretend you have a balloon tied to the top of your head, lifting your whole body straight up.
- **Are your ribs out of alignment with your hips?** If you're slouching or leaning to one side for too long, you can put unnecessary pressure on your back and muscles. Make sure your resting, default position is with your ribs directly over your hips, not leaning or jutting out in any direction.
- **Are your shoulders hunched forward, sagging downward, or uneven?** Set your shoulders above your hips, parallel and even, and keep your shoulder blades flat on your back. This will not only help you feel better physically; it can also help you feel more confident and capable.

- **Are your legs folded to one side, dangling toward the ground, or forcing your knees up above your hips when sitting?** If so, you might want to switch up the settings on your seat or try to make a few changes to your seated posture—especially if it's your chair at work or home or another chair you spend a lot of time in. Make sure your feet can rest flat on the floor in front of you and your knees are roughly level with your hips.

FIND AN EXERCISE THAT FITS YOUR NEEDS

Although it's a wonderful and worthwhile activity to work on accepting yourself as you are, it's not a bad thing to work on improving yourself. Most of us have at least one or two areas that we would like to improve.

For this exercise, focus on one area that you want to improve and define what change you want to see; for example, you might want to lose some weight around your midsection or tone up your backside.

Once you have your goal in mind, search online fitness websites or talk to a personal trainer or other fitness expert about what exercises will help you reach your goal.

To really make a noticeable difference, you'll probably need to add a few exercises to your repertoire, but pick one that you are most hopeful about and try it out right away. Once you realize that you can do it and it's not as complex or difficult as it might seem, you'll be extra motivated to keep going!

Let that motivation and feeling of accomplishment translate to a sense of bliss in your body and pride in your effort.

DO 1 MINUTE OF JUMPING JACKS

Getting your heart pumping can be a good way to enhance positive feelings both in your body and about your body.

To tap into those good feelings, set a timer for 1 minute and do some jumping jacks!

Here's how:

1. Stand with your legs straight and your arms at your sides.
2. In one smooth motion (or not-so-smooth motion—that's okay too!), hop straight up and bring your feet out wide and your hands up above your head.
3. In another smooth motion, hop up again and bring your arms and legs back to their starting positions, legs together and straight and arms at your sides.

Continue doing jumping jacks for the full minute. It's okay if you don't get many in during that time; whether you do five or fifty jumping jacks, just make sure you give it solid effort.

When the timer goes off, stop the jumping jacks and spend a few moments noticing how your body feels. You are probably sweaty and out of breath, but you might also feel exhilarated, energized, and just a bit more confident. Enjoy those feelings and revel in the slightly-tired-but-invigorated sensation in your muscles.

BOOK A MASSAGE

It might feel a little extravagant, especially if you don't typically spend money on non-essential things for yourself, but remember that it's okay to be a little extravagant on occasion! Your health and happiness are worth splurging on now and then.

Find a reputable massage parlor or spa near you and search through your options: a Swedish massage is the traditional feel-good massage, a deep-tissue massage is a good (but painful) way to tease out knots and release tension in your muscles, and a hot stone massage incorporates small, smooth stones heated to a warm, comfortable temperature to melt away stress.

If you're not too keen on the idea of a stranger rubbing you down or you don't have the funds for a professional massage, there are other options—see if you can cajole or persuade a friend or significant other to give you a short massage. If no one seems eager to give you a rub, there are always massaging chairs! The sensations aren't quite as good, but it can still feel luxurious and make you feel happy and blissful in your body.

PUT ON SOME POLISH

The ladies will probably find this exercise more relevant, but there's no law against men enjoying some nail polish too! If you don't really like the look of nail polish on your fingernails, use clear polish instead.

Set a few minutes of your busy day aside to make yourself feel pampered and blissful. Grab some pretty polish, cotton balls, and nail polish remover for any mistakes.

Wash your hands and use nail clippers or a file to prepare your nails to be painted, if necessary. Start off slowly and mindfully, paying attention to the sensations, smells, and visuals. Notice how satisfying it is to see a smooth coat of polish gradually covering the entire nail. Extend that satisfying feeling as you paint each nail on one hand, then switch to the other and continue putting on the first coat.

Give your nails a few minutes to dry slightly, use the nail polish remover to correct any mistakes, then start the second round of polish.

Once you've finished, spread your fingers out and inspect your hands. Notice how much a simple coat or two of polish can change up your look, and allow yourself to feel pretty, elegant, and pleased.

DROP AND GIVE YOURSELF TWENTY

If you really need a boost—to your energy level, your mood, or anything else—doing a quick physical exercise can be a great way to get it.

Find a spot on the floor that's clear (and preferably one that's relatively clean) and drop to your hands and knees. Next, follow these guidelines to ensure that you don't cheat yourself by doing half-hearted push-ups.

1. Try to keep your body as stiff and straight as possible; push your tailbone down (so your butt isn't sticking up) and keep your calves and thighs parallel to each other and to the ground (so your knees aren't bent).
2. Make sure your shoulders aren't drawn up toward your ears. Keep them in a natural position.
3. Keep your elbows in by your sides to ensure good posture all the way up and all the way down.
4. Fix your gaze on something a couple feet ahead of you on the ground so you're looking a bit ahead rather than straight down. This will help keep your neck in proper alignment.
5. Slowly allow yourself to move toward the ground, while keeping all of the above in mind; don't let your arms bow out or your butt float up toward the ceiling.

6. As you push yourself up again, try not to go too fast or in jerky motions. The ideal motion is a smooth one, with just a hint of a pause at the top. You can also pause at the bottom if you'd like to give your muscles an extra challenge.

Try to keep all of these in mind. I know it can be hard, but there's really no point in exercising if you're not doing it correctly. Improper exercise is a waste of your time, because you won't be reaping the benefits of your effort. Don't waste your own time, and honor your effort by committing to proper form!

If you can't drop and give yourself twenty, drop and give yourself ten. Or five. Or one. Or do an alternate version of a push-up, like at a different angle or with your knees on the ground. It doesn't really matter whether you can do push-ups or how many you can do; what matters is that you give solid effort to an activity that is good for you.

PLAY WITH A NEW HAIRSTYLE

Changing things up occasionally is healthy, fun, and can bring you a renewed sense of joy. If you usually stick to the same hairstyle every day, this is a great opportunity to mix things up and try a new look.

If you usually straighten your hair, grab a curler. If you usually curl your hair, fire up a straightener. For those who always wear their hair down, get some hair elastics and bobby pins and prepare to put it up. If you're low-maintenance when it comes to your hair, pull out some product and/or any kind of tool you have lying around.

Stand in front of the mirror and play with your look for a few minutes. Try something elegant and timeless, something bold and fresh, or something completely crazy. You don't have to wear it that way all day, but it's fun to use a little creativity on something that can be such a strict and boring routine.

Take a look in the mirror and admire your new look. Be grateful for all your options when it comes to how you present yourself to the world!

LOTION UP

There's only one step between you and an instant mini boost of bliss in your skin: some soft and silky moisturizer!

Most of us have at least a bottle or two of lotion lying around somewhere, and it's often just a quick hop down to the local drugstore or grocery store to pick some up if you're out. Grab some lotion and bare some skin, then follow these steps:

1. Start with a large area, like your legs or arms. Pour out a generous portion of lotion and start to gently and slowly work it into your skin.
2. As you spread the lotion over your skin, practice a bit of mindfulness; pay attention to how it feels as your skin drinks it in. Notice the sensations as you gently rub the lotion in.
3. Continue applying lotion wherever your skin is dry, cracked, or in need of some softening.
4. As you finish up, imagine that your skin was parched and dying for some moisture, and that it is grateful for the relief you just gave it.

Revel in your silky-smooth skin and enjoy the small sense of bliss that comes with it!

PUT ON YOUR FAVORITE OUTFIT

When you need a quick boost to your self-confidence or self-esteem, doing something as simple as trying on your favorite outfit can help—even if you only wear it for a few minutes and immediately change into something else again!

Your favorite outfit is your favorite for a reason—it makes you look good and feel good about yourself. In some cases, it can even act as a sort of mask or costume, helping you to put on the persona of someone who is more confident, someone more self-assured, or someone who seems exceedingly capable.

Drag your favorite pieces out of your closet and slip into them. Stand in front of the mirror in your best outfit and drink in the view. Let the confidence and self-esteem seep in and enjoy the boost to your self-assurance and body bliss!

Use this exercise to remind you of how it feels to have confidence in yourself and to remind yourself that you have the capacity to feel like that all the time. Your mind is the only thing holding you back!

PART 3

EXPERIENCE BLISS IN YOUR RELATIONSHIPS

WRITE A SHORT LETTER TO A LOVED ONE

Even if you don't send it, writing a heartfelt letter can do wonders for your mood and for your relationships. Follow these simple guidelines to give it a try:

1. Grab a pen and a piece of paper, sit down, and give yourself some time to write. Silence your phone and turn off the TV or radio to minimize distractions.
2. Think about whom you want to address your letter to—has anyone been particularly kind to you lately? Or perhaps you've felt a surge of love for a friend or family member recently? Whomever it is, just make sure to choose someone you love who loves you back.
3. Put all your good thoughts about this person on paper. Tell her about her positive qualities, what she means to you, how she has made you feel, and anything else that comes to mind.
4. Sign the letter with a loving closing (e.g., "With love" or "Yours truly") and your signature.

Whether you mail the letter or not, embrace the boost to your happiness and the enhanced sense of connection with your loved one.

PRACTICE GRATITUDE FOR THOSE YOU LOVE

One of the best ways to feel happier and more blissful is to cultivate gratitude and appreciation for what you already have, and some of the best things you already have to feel grateful for are your positive relationships.

To enhance your sense of relationship bliss and build your connection with those you love, try this gratitude exercise:

1. Think of one person you love deeply and write their name on a piece of paper or in your notebook or journal.
2. Underneath their name, list some concrete reasons why you are grateful for them. A reason might be "He sat through the night with me when my son was sick" or "She bought me groceries when I was completely broke a week before payday."
3. Once your list is complete (or at least really full), take a minute to read through it and practice your gratitude for each item on the list with this statement: "I am grateful to [*loved one's name*] for [*reason*]."

If you have more time, you can repeat this exercise for each loved one you are grateful for. Practice this at least once or twice a week to get maximum benefits.

CREATE A RELATIONSHIP MANTRA

If you're not familiar with mantras, don't worry—they're easy to understand and even easier to craft!

A mantra is a word, phrase, or short sentence that you repeat to yourself throughout your day in order to remind yourself of your intentions and facilitate a life that is compatible with your goals and values.

If you want to work on building up your relationships with others, a relationship mantra is a good way to do it.

To craft your own customized relationship mantra, use these tips as guidelines:

1. It should be short and to the point—no more than a few words or a succinct sentence.
2. It should be connected to the goal of building, maintaining, or strengthening your relationship(s).
3. It should remind you of your intention to enhance your relationship(s) and motivate you to live out that intention.

Some good examples might be:

- "I see the good in others and I treasure it."
- "I will have love and respect for all."
- "I strive for love—not superiority—in my relationships."

- "I remove the walls around myself."
- "The joy in me will perpetuate joy in others."
- "Today I will focus on the light in others and myself."

You might not feel like your mantra is true or relevant right now, but with enough practice it can be.

VIDEO CHAT WITH SOMEONE YOU LOVE

Sometimes a friend or family member's caring and compassionate voice can do wonders for your emotional state; however, those who live far away from their families will understand that sometimes it's just not possible to get that face-to-face interaction.

If you can't make a face-to-face meeting work, try using a video chat service to connect with your loved one. There are tons of programs, apps, and software packages out there that you can use to video chat, so you have a lot of options!

Take some time to figure out which one is best for you, how it works, and how to convince your loved one to get the same one. Once they have it up and running, set up a time to chat with your loved one.

It doesn't really matter what you talk about—you could talk about the weather, your work, your relationship, or a million other things—what matters is that you connect or reconnect with your loved one, see their face, and engage on a deeper level than texting or calling can provide.

SEND SOMEONE A PRAYER OR GOOD VIBES

Whether you are deeply religious, completely secular, or somewhere in between, you can find incredible peace and contentment in saying a prayer or sending out good thoughts or "vibes" for someone. You don't need to believe in a higher power to find comfort and joy in putting your thoughts and well wishes out into the universe!

To bring yourself an extra bit of bliss or boost your connection with someone you love, try this exercise:

1. Think of a person you love and would like to either reconnect with or strengthen your bond with.
2. Come up with one or two things you wish for this person, like a speedy recovery from an illness or an extra dose of confidence for a job interview.
3. Come up with a prayer or "I wish for him/her..." statements that capture your hopes for your loved one.
4. Gather up all your love for this person and send your prayer or wish statements out into the universe.

As you'll notice after completing this exercise, it feels great to think kindly and lovingly of others, and even better to put your well wishes into words!

CUDDLE UP WITH A PET

As you probably know, spending time with your furry friend can have significant benefits. It can make you happier, reduce symptoms of depression and anxiety, and even improve your physical health! Take advantage of these excellent benefits by spending a few minutes cuddling with your pet.

If you don't have a pet at home, think about someone in your life who does: do your parents, siblings, or children have pets? How about a good friend or neighbor? Chances are, you know someone with a friendly pet who would be happy to loan them out to you for a few minutes.

In the 5 minutes you commit to spending with your pet, focus on giving and receiving love. Most healthy, happy pets have a lot of love to give, and they're usually thrilled to get some back! Think about really making a connection with your pet through each touch. Look your pet in the eyes and enjoy the bonding.

Make sure you don't slip into absentminded petting or mindless play; keep your focus on the warm, fuzzy connection between you and your pet, and you'll get a rush of good feelings to go with it!

TRY A LOVING-KINDNESS MEDITATION

Loving-kindness meditation is a special type of meditation that you can use to feel more connected and positive about yourself, your loved ones, acquaintances, strangers, and eventually even all beings in the universe.

To give this meditation a try, follow these steps:

1. **Sit in a comfortable position, close your eyes, and start to focus on your breathing.** Don't try to change it at first; just observe it and notice the sensations as you breathe.
2. **Begin to breathe in and out from your "heart center,"** or the center of your lower chest/upper abdominal area. Direct your inhales to it and expel your exhales from it.
3. **Cultivate a feeling of deep love**—unconditional, unassuming, irrepressible, and without expectations. Let it grow and expand from a tiny seed into a cloud big enough to envelop you. Direct this feeling toward yourself first, offering yourself this wonderful gift of loving-kindness.
4. **Next, expand this deep love even more and radiate it out toward the people you love**—your partner or significant other, your children, other family members, and your dearest and most cherished friends.

5. **Once it has reached out to all those you love, expand it once again** and allow it to radiate even further and touch your acquaintances, people you know *of* but don't actually know, and total strangers.

6. **This next step is the hardest, but it's one of the most important things you can do for your own well-being and bliss:** expand your deep love to be even broader and allow it to touch even those you dislike or despise. It may not be easy, and it probably won't feel natural, but with practice you will find yourself able to empathize with and extend your loving-kindness to even those you have little to no love for.

7. **Finally, take this love and extend it to every single being in the universe.** Wish for love, happiness, health, and well-being for all.

8. **Open your eyes and smile!**

LIST THREE REASONS TO LOVE THEM

When you keep the importance of your relationships and your many reasons for loving your friends and family in mind, you will find it much easier to see the joy in those relationships.

To boost your relationships with your loved ones and open yourself up to greater bliss, try listing three reasons to love them.

Grab a notebook or your journal. Open it up to a new page and write the name of someone you love dearly at the top. Next, write down three unique reasons why you love him or her.

For example, you might write your spouse's name at the top of the page and list reasons like:

1. She is a great listener and always there to hear me out, whether I'm complaining, rejoicing, grumbling, or chattering on at a mile a minute.
2. She has the most beautiful smile and she lights up the room with her laughter—and she laughs a lot!
3. She is a caring person who would do anything to help her family or friends, even giving them the clothes off her back.

Reflect on these reasons and allow yourself to love the person even more deeply than before.

CALL UP A FRIEND

Talking to a close friend can be uplifting, motivating, and bliss-inducing. It often doesn't even matter what they say—just hearing their voice can do the trick.

For this exercise, the first step is to pick a friend. He or she should be:

1. Close to you (emotionally, not physically).
2. Someone you trust and enjoy spending time with.
3. Someone who understands and appreciates the drive to improve oneself (which you are engaging by reading this book!).

Once you have your friend in mind, all you need to do is give him a call! If you think it will help direct your conversation, you can tell your friend why you are calling; however, that is not a necessary part of the exercise.

If you don't tell your friend you are calling as part of a mood-enhancing, self-improvement exercise, just make sure you don't act as if you're calling him for a certain reason, like needing his help with something or asking a specific question. Just call to chat and enjoy the conversation!

MAKE A NEW FRIEND

This exercise must be practiced in a public place, since it requires you to find and interact with a complete stranger! To minimize any potential awkwardness, pick a situation that has a lot of conversation and at least some milling and mingling, like drinking at a bar, standing in a line for a fun event, or hanging out at a busy park.

Look around you and find one person with at least some sort of connection to you. It could be what they're wearing, what they're doing, their topic of conversation, or any other connection.

Once you've decided whom to talk to, either approach them right away or wait for an opportune moment, like when their friends walk away or you catch each other's eye. Introduce yourself to this person and point out your connection (e.g., "Hey, I love your shirt. That's my favorite show too!").

Try to pick someone who seems friendly and open to conversation, and respectfully walk away if they don't feel like talking to you.

Attempting to make a new friend can be terrifying, but you'll find that it's totally worth it when you put yourself out there.

PERFORM A RANDOM ACT OF KINDNESS

You know how doing something nice for someone else makes you feel? Sort of warm and gooey inside and full to the brim with love? That's no accident—doing something good for another person is one of the quickest and most effective ways to boost your own bliss!

To get in on that boost, try doing one random act of kindness right now. It can be for anyone, from your spouse to a complete stranger, and it can be anonymous or direct and in person. The specifics don't matter beyond these three guidelines:

1. It must benefit someone else in a meaningful way, and it must not harm anyone else.
2. It must not be in return for something or for a specific occasion, like exchanging gifts or celebrating something special with a loved one.
3. It must take you 5 minutes or less to accomplish.

That's it! That's all you need to do. Simply find someone you'd like to do something nice for, make sure it's a random act of kindness, and do it in 5 minutes or less.

If you're not sure what to do, try paying for a stranger's order at the drive-through.

COMMIT TO AUTHENTICITY

When you are authentically "you," you are happier, healthier, and open to more bliss. You are also more comfortable and secure in your relationships when you know that your loved ones understand and appreciate the real you.

To reap the benefits of being authentically you, try this exercise.

Sit quietly and take a few deep breaths to get centered. Ask yourself:

1. Who am I?
2. What do I want?
3. How does it feel to be me?

If you're not sure how to answer these questions, don't worry—you're not alone! It's perfectly normal to feel a bit lost trying to come up with answers. The journey to answering these questions is how you figure out who you are.

As you think about the answers, make sure they are not tinged with thoughts of who you *should* be, who others want you to be, or how you would best fit in with those around you.

Keep your answers to these questions in mind, even if they're only half-formed, and check in often to make sure you are acting in accordance with your own personal values.

NOTE ONE POSITIVE THING
ABOUT EVERYONE YOU SEE

When you see the best in others, you get better at seeing the best in yourself too. And when you see the best in yourself, you find it much easier to stay positive and upbeat!

To practice seeing the best in others and in yourself, give this exercise a try:

1. Look around you and notice each person you see. If you're in a crowded place with lots of people nearby, choose the closest five or six people.
2. For each person, note one positive thing about them. Examples of positive things include a nice scarf a person is wearing, a small act of kindness you witness, or seeing someone being a good parent by playing with their child.
3. Think about how easy it is to miss each of these things if you're not really keeping an eye out for it. Appreciate the positive moments you got to see and acknowledge that you wouldn't have seen them if you weren't actively looking for them.

Enjoy the mood boost this exercise brings, and remember to practice it again soon to make it a habit.

CREATE A RELATIONSHIP WEB

If you're one of those people who finds things easier to understand and appreciate when there's a good visual, you'll love this exercise. It will help you identify the most important relationships in your life and remind you of all the people who make you happy.

Grab your journal or notebook and a pen, flip to a new page, and follow these steps:

1. In the center of the page draw a circle and write "Me."
2. Draw four or five concentric circles around the center that gradually increase in size as they move away from the center.
3. Think about the most important people in your life. Make a list of them if that helps your thought process and put the relationships in order of importance.
4. Take the first name on your list, the person whose relationship is most vital to you, and draw a small circle for them somewhere between yours and the first concentric circle. Write their name in the circle.
5. Repeat step 4 with the next name on your list, but be sure to place it somewhere that makes sense in relation to the first name (e.g., if the first two names are your parents, their circles would be right next to each other).

6. Continue placing circles until you have placed one for every name on your list.
7. Stand back and take a look at the finished product: a relationship web that represents all the most important people in your life, how close they are to you, and how they relate with the other important people in your life.

This visual representation of the love in your life will remind you of how much love there is around you and prompt you to value and appreciate these relationships even more. Look back on it whenever you feel lonely or need a reminder that you are loved, and allow yourself to be filled with the love you see displayed on the page.

Keep in mind that the web doesn't need to be exact; you don't need to get out a ruler to ensure that the distances are accurate! It's meant to be simply a rough approximation of the love that fills your life.

ENJOY A MEANINGFUL HUG

What feels better than a warm, loving hug? Not much!

Human contact is so important for our happiness and well-being—even more important than we might think. In the days of social media and video chatting, it's all too easy to spend a ton of time away from our loved ones and feel that keen lack of human touch.

To ensure that you give yourself some of the best opportunities for bliss in your life, try sharing a meaningful hug with someone you love.

The person you choose for this exercise doesn't need to be your spouse or your best friend, but they should be someone whom you feel happy and comfortable around.

Ask this person if you can give them a good hug and explain that a good hug involves a prolonged embrace and a mindful focus on the act of hugging. Make sure your hugging partner is okay with a long, touchy-feely hug, and go for it!

While you embrace your friend or loved one, think about their best traits, your favorite memories with them, and anything else about them that makes you smile, and ask them to do the same.

GIVE SOMEONE A SMOOCH

There's a reason why people all over the world engage in kissing—it's a natural and satisfying behavior that helps you feel closer to those you love and more invested in your relationships (and frequently acts as the precursor to some other intimate bonding behaviors!).

When choosing a loved one to smooch, make sure you pick someone you share a warm relationship with, someone who would be comfortable receiving a kiss, and someone whom you *want* to kiss. This person might be someone you kiss romantically, like your spouse or significant other, but it could also be someone you would give a more platonic smooch to, like a close friend or family member.

Pick your special someone and make sure to get their permission first, then smooch away! Bookend the kiss with a couple of hugs. While hugging your loved one, think about how much they mean to you and how much you appreciate your warm relationship. Thank them for the kiss and bask in the warm, fuzzy glow of bliss in your relationship.

ENGAGE IN PROLONGED EYE CONTACT

This might be awkward at first, but it's an excellent way to enhance your connection with someone you love. Try this exercise with someone you are very close with, and make sure they're on board with it too—it can get intense, and you don't want to make anyone uncomfortable.

Explain to your loved one that this exercise is simple, involving only sustained eye contact for a few minutes. When they agree to give it a shot, get out your phone or watch and set the timer to 3 minutes.

Sit comfortably and look into each other's eyes, holding eye contact for the full 3 minutes. You can either allow your thoughts to drift wherever they will, or you can set an intention to think only positive thoughts about your loved one.

Whichever option you choose, you will probably find that your thoughts naturally drift to positive things about your loved one. Holding eye contact for a prolonged period of time is an extremely intimate act, and it can bring up strong feelings of love and help you find joy in the other person. Embrace that bliss and allow it to fill you up.

SAY YOU'RE SORRY

Making mistakes is an inevitable part of life, but there is a silver lining—the positive, uplifting, and downright blissful experience that apologizing and making amends can be.

Think of something you need to apologize for. It doesn't need to be something monumental or life-changing; it could be as simple as missing a friend's birthday party after you committed to attend or inadvertently making a mean or offensive remark.

When you apologize, make sure to:

- Actually use the word *sorry* or *apologize*.
- Be sincere.
- Be honest.
- Don't make excuses.
- Tell them how much they mean to you.
- Ask if there is anything you can do to make amends.

We've all received one of those apologies that sounds like the person is apologizing, but really they are simply justifying, blaming, making excuses, or minimalizing the situation. Those types of apologies are not effective because they don't resolve the issue and no one feels better in the end. A good apology, on the other hand, is one that acknowledges what you did wrong, explains why it was wrong, promises that you'll try to do differently in the future, and includes a request for forgiveness.

Apologizing when you have wronged somebody can help you rebuild or enhance your connection with them, and it just plain feels good. It takes a load off your mind and your heart when you acknowledge your mistakes and do what you can to fix them, and it can even induce a sense of bliss.

After completing this exercise, you might find you have an urge to keep going—indulge that urge to take a load off your mind and experience bliss!

TELL SOMEONE YOU LOVE THEM—
AND TELL THEM WHY

It's wonderful to hear that someone loves you, no matter what kind of love that is. Luckily, it also feels wonderful to tell someone you love them! Take advantage of this win-win and boost your bliss by telling someone you love them—but kick it up a notch by also telling them *why* you love them.

Pick someone who is important to you but with whom you may not always be vocal in sharing your love. Come up with at least three reasons why you love this person, like:

1. She has a great sense of humor and is always making you laugh.
2. He is incredibly generous to everyone and is always willing to share what he has with those less fortunate.
3. She fights fairly—without name-calling, insults, or the intention to wound.

Once you have your list of reasons, share them with your loved one. You can do this however feels most natural to you, but you can also use this script if you're not sure how to go about it:

"Hey, I just wanted to let you know how much you mean to me. I love you, and here's why…"

REFLECT ON YOURSELF AS A PARTNER

Just as it's important to reflect on yourself and on your relationships with others, it's vital to reflect on yourself as a partner. The only way to improve is to know *where* you can improve, and reflection is one of the best ways to figure that out.

Take some time to think about your most important or closest relationship. This is likely your relationship with your spouse or significant other, but it may also be your relationship with a best friend, a parent, or a child.

Ask yourself these three questions:

1. What am I like as a partner?
2. Would I want to date/be friends with/be closely related to me?
3. What are my best qualities as a partner and what can I do to enhance or strengthen them?

You will probably want to record your answers to these questions in a notebook or journal so you can look back on them later. As you write them down, commit to answering these questions honestly and don't shy away from the truth or be overly modest.

Use your answers to become the best possible partner you can be, bringing bliss to yourself and to those you love.

TAKE A HIGH-LEVEL VIEW

If you sometimes find it difficult to keep your head above the messy, often chaotic reality of life, it might help to take a high-level view. It's much easier to find bliss when you're not focusing on the little things that simply don't matter that much!

To take a high-level view, follow these steps:

1. **Think about a fight you recently had with a loved one over something relatively small.** It shouldn't be something huge, like arguing over deeply held beliefs, but something like forgetting to take out the trash—*again*.
2. **See the disagreement or argument in your mind's eye.** Take a view from above and see you and your loved one in the midst of your disagreement.
3. **Slowly zoom out until you see your whole home.** Think about how wonderful it is to have a home and to share it with someone you love!
4. **Zoom out a bit more until you see your whole neighborhood.** Think about all the little disagreements and arguments that people have all through the neighborhood, and realize that yours was but one tiny blip on the radar.
5. **Zoom out even farther so you have a bird's-eye view of the whole town or city where you live.** Think about all the places you and

your loved one have been together and how many things you've done together, especially those that created fond memories.

6. **Zoom out one final time to see the whole country, then the whole world.** Try to see your little corner of the world in your mind's eye from this level and realize that you can't! Think about how lucky you are to have your loved one in your life, and how lucky it was to find them in this huge sea of over seven billion people.

Now that you've zoomed all the way out, think about how important that little issue was in the grand scheme of things. It probably seems pretty small! Since it's so small, it's easy enough to let go of it and focus on what's really important: your love for this person.

When you finish the exercise, go to your loved one (or text them if that's not feasible) and tell them how much you love them. Find common ground on the disagreement and, in doing so, find some bliss.

COMMIT TO IMPROVING YOUR RELATIONSHIPS AND MAKE A PLAN

If you completed the earlier "Reflect On Yourself As a Partner" exercise and realized that you do have some areas that could use improvement, or if you've received some feedback on how you can improve your relationships with others, use this exercise to guide your steps.

Here's what to do:

1. Think about *why* you want to improve your relationships. How would improving your relationships affect your life and the lives of those you love?
2. Think about *how* you can improve your relationships. Are there things you can stop doing, start doing, or do differently? Write them down.
3. Commit to following through on the behaviors you outlined in step 2. Write that commitment down too.
4. Come up with a plan to implement these changes. It doesn't need to be too long, but it should include some concrete actions you will take (e.g., "I will use active listening when talking to my wife and my children").
5. Follow through on your plan and be consistent.

It isn't rocket science—improving your relationships just takes a little time and effort—and the extra bliss you will find as a result will make the effort more than worth it!

USE ACTIVE LISTENING

Active listening is an incredibly useful technique that helps you improve your connections with others and experience more bliss in your life and in your relationships. When you use active listening, you are showing respect for the other person's feelings and point of view, which in turn will help that person open up more about the problem at hand. In addition, when someone feels like they are being listened to attentively, there is less chance of the conflict getting heated or out of control and it often results in a a quicker resolution of the problem.

To practice active listening, keep these guidelines in mind when someone is speaking to you:

- Make sure you are giving the speaker your *full* attention.
- Show the speaker that you are listening with feedback like maintaining eye contact, nodding and smiling, and sending small verbal messages that correspond to what they're saying.
- Practice patience and don't interrupt; let them speak until it seems like they have finished their thought (e.g., they paused for a few seconds and looked to you for a response).
- Remain as neutral and objective as possible instead of taking sides or jumping on the bandwagon.

- Listen closely to what they are saying rather than half-listening while crafting a rebuttal or relevant anecdote in your head.
- Ask insightful questions and paraphrase what they said to you when it's your turn to speak.

The more you practice active listening, the happier you (and your conversation partners) will be!

SHARE SOMETHING NEW

Do you remember that phase in a new relationship (of any kind, but especially close friendships and romantic relationships) where you talk all the time, thrilled to be learning so much about one another? That excitement about the other person is a huge source of bliss in new relationships, but it can still be stimulated in older, longer-term relationships as well.

When you are with your partner and find yourself out of things to say or even enjoying a comfortable, companionable silence, share something new with them. This new thing must be:

1. True and honest.
2. Something your partner has not heard before.
3. An engaging conversation starter, revealing something unexpected, impressive, or humorous about yourself.

This exercise gets harder to do the longer you've been with someone, but it is always possible! Even the closest couples have at least some sort of life that is separate from their significant other, even if it's mostly in their own head.

Give this exercise a try to feel a rush of relationship bliss and be reminded of your exciting early days together!

LEAVE A KIND MESSAGE

Doing something kind for others can be an excellent way to share bliss and feel more blissful ourselves.

Think about someone in your life who could use a little pick-me-up or a reminder that they are a good and valuable person. Decide on your "target" for this exercise and figure out the best way to leave them a message.

There are a ton of options for leaving this person a kind message: you can go the old-fashioned route and leave them a handwritten note where they will find it, the not-quite-as-old-fashioned method of calling and leaving a voice mail, or one of the many other ways to send someone a message: texting, email, a messaging app like iMessage or Snapchat, and so on.

However you decide to do it, make sure the message:

- Is kind.
- Is honest.
- Is completely unbidden (e.g., not about anything else).
- Does not ask for anything in return.
- Is designed to make the receiver feel good.

Have some fun with this exercise and enjoy the rush of bliss it gives you!

ASK FOR WHAT YOU NEED

For some reason, a lot of us have a hard time telling others what we need or how we want them to treat us. It might feel awkward, but asking for what we need is a foundational aspect of effective communication and successful relationships.

Think about it this way: don't you always want to give your partner what they need in your relationship? Wouldn't it be nice if they just outright *told you* what they need?

If your answer is "Yes," give this exercise a try.

1. First, think about which (if any) of your needs are not being fully met.
2. Next, brainstorm some ways your partner or loved one could help you meet those needs and fill in the gaps.
3. Finally, speak to your partner and gently tell them that, although they are wonderful and appreciated, there are some ways they could up their relationship game and help you feel even happier! Any good partner will be thrilled to say, "Yes" and make small but meaningful changes.

Share your needs and ideas with them, allow them to bounce some ideas off you if they'd like to, and share the bliss that results with one another.

ASK YOUR PARTNER WHAT THEY NEED

Just as it's vital for your partner to know what you need, it's also vital to know what your partner needs. The best relationships are built on a solid foundation of respect, honesty, and communication.

To foster each of these three cornerstones of successful relationships, take the initiative and ask your partner what they need from you.

If you're not sure how to go about it, you can use this short script to guide the discussion:

"[Partner], I really care about you and I want to make sure we nurture our relationship. Is there anything you need that I'm not doing? Is there anything I could improve or do more of to make you feel more loved, cared for, and understood?"

Just as important as asking these questions is truly listening to the answers and considering what your partner says they need. Reflect what you heard back at them to make sure you understand them.

Finally, come up with a plan (in your head or with your partner) to make sure you are giving your partner what they need. They will appreciate it, and you will find your relationship much improved, making it easier to experience joy with your partner.

ELEVATE YOUR NEXT SHARED MEAL

Even if you're not into the sophistication (or snobbery) of fine dining, it's nice to occasionally make a meal with your partner extra special.

For your next shared meal, make sure you're prepared. Here are a few things that can take a simple meal from "business as usual" to "romantic meal for two":

- Slightly dim lighting and candles (tall candles are elegant, but any will do).
- A tablecloth. It's just a piece of fabric, but it's amazing how it can transform a dining area!
- An actual place setting. Instead of just tossing a knife and a fork onto a plate, set your table like a nice restaurant would.
- Soft music to set the mood.
- If you want to make it really special, get some fresh-cut flowers to use as a centerpiece.

These are all simple things (and relatively cheap or easy to include) but put together, they can make a big impact on your partner.

Show him how special he is to you and how much you love him, and you will create space for profound joy and bliss in your relationship.

EXCHANGE "THIS IS ME" PLAYLISTS

Art is not only a wonderful medium of entertainment; it's also a great way to express ourselves and connect with one another. We frequently hear things like "That movie is my life in a nutshell" or "That song is my anthem." We identify with art, often on an intensely personal level.

Use this connection to art to your advantage and get to know someone better through music.

Create a "This Is Me" playlist that includes your favorite artists, your favorite songs, and songs that you feel perfectly capture who you are and what you care about.

Once you have a playlist put together, share it with your partner or friend to get to know each other better. Set aside some time to listen to each song carefully, looking up the lyrics if necessary to really understand each one.

When you have both listened to each other's playlists, get together and discuss. Notice any similarities and differences, point out common themes, and dive a little bit deeper into anything you don't totally "get."

The enhanced connection that results from this exercise is sure to boost the joy you experience in your relationship.

TRADE FAVORITE MOVIES

Someone's favorite movie can (theoretically) tell you a lot about them—do they prefer to laugh or spend more time deep in thought? Are they passionate about a cause? Do they enjoy thrilling tales or harrowing dramas? This exercise is one good way to find out!

Pick your favorite movie (or one of your favorite movies if you have several) and ask your partner or loved one to do the same. Exchange the movies with one another and agree to watch the other person's favorite sometime in the near future.

Later, when you find the time to watch the movie, stay focused and mindful, taking in each moment of this movie that means so much to your partner. Meet up again, ready to discuss the movie in depth.

If you take advantage of this opportunity, it's almost guaranteed that a more blissful relationship will follow. As a final note, know that movies are a good choice for this activity, but you could also use songs, poems, short stories, sculptures, photographs, or anything else that you connect deeply with.

SET HEALTHY BOUNDARIES—AND ENFORCE THEM

One of the best ways to ensure that you and your loved ones have healthy relationships full of love, respect, and bliss is to set some healthy boundaries.

Boundaries are important to ensure that you are not giving too much of yourself and that you have limits on how much you can take, even (or especially) from those you love the most.

To come up with some healthy boundaries, grab your notebook or a piece of paper and something to write with and write two headings next to each other on the page:

- Things I Expect
- Things I Will Not Tolerate

Under the first heading, write things like "Respect from my partner" and "Consideration of my feelings."

Under the second heading, write things like "Ignoring my explicit requests" and "Lying to me."

Think about what these boundaries mean and come up with some scenarios where they would come into play. If you commit to enforcing these healthy boundaries, you can rest secure in the knowledge that you have set your relationships up for success—and what's a more blissful feeling than that?

DO SOMETHING NEW TOGETHER

Doing something new on your own can be exciting, exhilarating, and growth-inducing, and so can doing something new with someone you love—but trying it out together offers another valuable benefit: it can improve your connection and bring you both more bliss as well!

Talk to your partner about what you can do together that's new and fresh. See if there's something she has always wanted to try, like taking a French cooking class, going parasailing, or taking a salsa dancing class.

Tell your partner about things you've been wanting to try as well, and hopefully you can find something you are both interested in doing!

Before ending the conversation, decide on at least one new thing to do together and commit to it, whether that involves signing up, putting down a deposit, or just scheduling some time into your calendars.

Enjoy the anticipation of your upcoming activity and savor the feelings of joy and bliss as you try something brand-new!

PLAN A TRIP WITH SOMEONE YOU LOVE

Obviously you can't take a trip in just 5 minutes, but you can start making plans for a fun trip in that amount of time!

Talk to your partner or loved one about an upcoming trip: to see some friends get married, visit family, or go on vacation to a popular travel destination. Whatever the reason or place, tell your loved one that you'd like to use this trip as a way to work on building an even better relationship.

Spend a few minutes talking about what you both would like to do on this trip, plan out your time off work, and coordinate your schedules.

As time allows, you can start making more concrete plans, one piece at a time. Just make sure to keep each other in the loop and agree on the major points of your travels!

Taking a trip with someone you love is a great opportunity to improve your connection, try new things together, and boost your bliss.

CREATE A "WANTS AND NEEDS" LIST FOR YOUR POTENTIAL PARTNER

If you're single, this exercise is a great way to work on the quality of your relationship even before it begins. If you're clear on what you want and need in a partner, you're more likely to actively seek out and appreciate someone with those qualities.

Take a few minutes to think about what kind of relationship you want to have. Think about the traits and qualities your partner will have, what you will do together, and what your shared life will be like.

Grab a pen and a sheet of paper and divide it into two columns: "Wants" and "Needs."

In the "Wants" column, put things that you'd like to have in a relationship but that are not necessarily deal breakers. For instance, you might want a partner who agrees with you on politics or also prioritizes traveling above material things.

In the "Needs" column, write down those things you won't compromise on. These might include conflict resolution procedures, the decision to have children or not, or having compatible religious beliefs.

Now you have a great starting point to help you refine your search for a partner, which will help you choose someone who inspires your bliss.

VISUALIZE YOUR PARTNER'S JOY

Visualization is a powerful tool that you can use to get a clearer head, boost your motivation, and feel more bliss in your life. There is no limit to the things you can visualize, but this particular exercise will add another benefit to the list: improving your connection with your partner or other loved one.

When you have a few quiet moments to yourself, close your eyes and visualize your partner. If you are single, visualize someone else close to you, like a parent, a dear friend, or a sibling. See them clearly.

Once you have a good image in mind, visualize them receiving good news or doing something they really enjoy. Basically, visualize them doing anything that brings them an insane amount of joy.

Watch as their face lights up and their smile broadens, and open your ears to drink in their laughter. Revel in their joy as they revel in it, and let it fill you with the bliss that comes from seeing those you love happy.

Open your eyes, but carry that image with you and commit to bringing it into reality by doing something to make your partner that joyful.

HOLD HANDS AND
CHAT ABOUT YOUR DAY

The simplest pleasures in life can also be the most profound and the most important. One such simple pleasure is feeling close and connected to your partner for a few minutes, both physically and mentally/emotionally.

At the end of your workday or when you climb into bed at night, set aside 5 minutes to just sit or lie next to one another, connect physically, and tell each other about your day.

You don't need to talk about any particularly weighty topics (unless you want to!); you can chat about interesting things you saw, heard, or did, share what your day was like, or talk about anything that came up over the course of your day.

You also don't need to be pressed against each other from head to toe (again, unless you want to, of course!); a small connection like holding hands can be effective in helping you feel in touch with one another.

In fact, the simple act of holding hands does a variety of bliss-boosting things:

- It relives stress
- It boosts love and bonding
- It lowers your blood pressure

- It fights fear and relieves pain
- It provides a sense of security and comfort

Taking just 5 minutes to make a small physical and emotional connection will give you an enduring sense of bliss in your relationship with your partner.

SHIFT YOUR SOURCE OF VALIDATION

All too often, we come to rely on others to validate us. It's a common occurrence, so don't feel bad if this describes you! The way forward is to shift the source of your validation from others to your inner self.

Here are some suggestions and guidelines to help you get started in just a few minutes:

1. **Identify your current sources of validation;** they might include your partner, your parents, your boss, or someone else in a position of (real or imagined) authority in your life.
2. **Remind yourself that while it's great to get the approval and validation of those you care about and respect,** true validation can only come from within.
3. **Acknowledge that your own inner self is the most important source of information about yourself,** including whether you are valid, loveable, and worthy.
4. **Open yourself up to hearing your inner voice and listen to what it says.** Your inner voice is supportive and encouraging, so if the voice you hear is neither of those things, dig a little deeper.

Practice this shifting of validation often—aim for at least once a day—and you can't help but experience more bliss!

GIVE SOME OF YOUR BLISS AWAY

One of the wonderful things about bliss is that it's not a zero-sum game; by giving some of your bliss to others, you don't actually take any away from yourself! Bliss multiplies; it never divides.

In a few spare minutes during your day, commit to sharing your bliss with someone else. Here are a few ways you might go about giving your bliss away:

- Smile at a stranger who seems down and, if they're open to it, start a conversation with them. Give them a compliment, remind them of something good, or simply listen attentively to give them a taste of bliss.
- Do something nice for a coworker for no particular reason, and do it anonymously.
- Pay for the order of the person behind you in the drive-through line.
- Remind your partner of something you love about him or her, randomly and without any precursor.
- Share a great tip on how to boost bliss with someone who needs it (perhaps a tip straight out of this book?).

The more you give your bliss away, the more bliss you'll have to work with.

SPEND YOUR EXTRA CASH ON SOMEONE ELSE

Although we all love to save up and spoil ourselves occasionally, studies have found that spending our money on others may have the best return on investment when it comes to happiness and bliss.

Instead of saving up to get that new gadget or toy you've been eyeing, try giving some of your money away instead. Here are a few good options, but feel free to send money wherever it can make the biggest impact:

- Donate it to a friend's GoFundMe campaign for a worthy cause.
- Give it to a friend who is getting back on her feet after a setback.
- Buy your spouse or significant other a gift you know he or she will absolutely love.
- Get your parents a random gift to show your gratitude for putting up with you during your teenage years.
- Pay for a stranger's oil change at the dealership or auto repair shop.
- Take an old friend out to dinner and cover the check.

These are just a few of the many, many ways you can find bliss by spending your money on others. Add your own ideas to the list so you have a lot of options for boosting your bliss!

REAPPRAISE YOUR ROMANTIC RELATIONSHIP

If you're looking to find more bliss in your current relationship with your partner, reappraisal is a great way to do it.

We know that getting some perspective and seeing things from new angles will do us good and help us make good decisions, but this is easier said than done. To learn how to get some perspective, try these steps:

1. Think about the biggest disagreement you have had with your partner lately (i.e., in the past few months).
2. Write about it from the perspective of an objective and truly neutral third party—one who hopes to come up with the most agreeable solution for all.
3. Write about the disagreement with a focus on any challenges that might hinder you from taking the above perspective in such a disagreement with your partner.
4. Finally, write down some best practices for implementing this objective, neutral third-party perspective during your disagreements.

Keeping an open mind and focusing on being objective, neutral, and fair during disagreements or conflicts with your partner can substantially improve the quality of your relationship, opening you both up to experiencing more bliss.

THANK YOUR PARTNER—
FOR SOMETHING THEY DO ALL THE TIME

This exercise is truly as simple as it sounds—all you need to do is tell your partner "thank you!"

The part that makes this exercise unique and more effective than simply thanking your partner for anything is the emphasis on thanking her for something she does *regularly*. It's surprisingly easy to forget to appreciate your partner for the things she does all the time.

To cultivate gratitude for your partner and bliss in your relationship, try this:

1. Think about something your partner always does and has done for a long time, like taking out the trash cans every week and bringing them back in, checking the mail, or paying the electric bill.
2. Thank your partner for doing this activity or task that she *always* does.
3. Watch her expression go from neutral to slightly confused to extremely pleased!

Everyone likes to be thanked for their efforts, especially when they feel their effort is not really noticed or particularly appreciated. Show your partner otherwise and share your gratitude with her, as well as the boost of bliss that follows.

LOOK AT THINGS FROM THEIR POINT OF VIEW

Whether you want to improve your relationship with a partner, friend, or anyone else, looking at things from their point of view will help you do that.

To see things from another person's perspective, follow these guidelines:

1. Think of a recent misunderstanding or disagreement you had with this person. Consider what it looked like from your perspective and note the details.
2. Now, flip the script: think about what that same disagreement looked like from their point of view. Imagine what they thought about the disagreement and try to understand their perspective on it.
3. Once you have a handle on how they *thought* about the disagreement, extend your empathy to how they *felt* about the disagreement. Consider how it felt to be in their shoes.

Now that you have a general idea of what they thought and felt, discuss it with them. Tell them you wanted to see things from their point of view and that you think you understand it better now. Describe it to them and see how well your idea matches up with reality.

Enhanced understanding and connection will make your relationship more conducive to shared bliss.

PLAN A CELEBRATION FOR YOUR LOVED ONE'S SUCCESS

We all love to be recognized for our achievements and celebrated for our success, especially when it comes from someone we love and respect. Take a few minutes to plan out exactly that for someone you love.

Pick someone you want to show your love for or someone who could use a little bit of celebrating right now. Think about what that person has done lately that warrants a celebration; it doesn't have to be something huge—it could be something relatively small, like passing another semester in college or successfully learning a new skill.

Consider how your loved one likes to celebrate; does he like to go all out with a party? Is he more of a "quiet dinner with family" sort of person? Somewhere in between? Decide on what kind of celebration his success warrants and what he would enjoy.

Based on the type of celebration you have decided on, take a few minutes to plan something fun to say "congratulations!"

Of course, make sure you follow through on it after planning it—that's the best part! Watch his eyes light up and bask in his bliss.

SURPRISE YOUR PARTNER— FOR NO REASON AT ALL

Note: you might want to use your best judgment for this one; some people *do not* like surprises, even good ones! However, most people are okay with small, pleasant surprises. If you've been thinking about showing your partner just how much you love her, this is the exercise for you.

Take a moment to think about what makes your partner happy: does she enjoy a certain food? A certain type of flower or candy? Is she dying to see a certain movie or try a new restaurant?

Based on your consideration of what she would enjoy, pick a small surprise for her: you might bring home her favorite food for dinner, pick up a bouquet of her favorite flowers or a box of her favorite candy, buy tickets to that movie, or make a reservation at that new restaurant.

Whatever you decide to surprise her with, keep it to yourself until the right moment! A popular choice is a few minutes after she gets home from work or just after she wakes up on a lazy weekend morning. Absorb her happiness when you surprise her and enjoy your shared boost of bliss.

REMIND YOUR PARTNER OF A SHARED LAUGH

Sharing laughter is a fabulous way of boosting your connection with your partner, and boosting your connection with your partner will naturally lead to more blissful feelings!

To boost your connection and open yourself up to greater bliss in your relationship, start by making a brief list of the times you have laughed the hardest or longest with your partner. Your list might look something like this:

- The time the waiter spilled iced tea all over him at the restaurant.
- How funny that grumpy old lady at the bed and breakfast was.
- When he came up with that great, unexpected one-liner at the party.

Your list doesn't have to be super descriptive, because you're just using it as a jumping-off point. Pick the two or three that you think caused the most laughter and joy.

Remind your partner of those funny instances. If he doesn't remember, paint a vivid picture so he can relive the experience and laugh until he cries all over again.

Laugh together, have fun together, and make *new* funny memories together, and you are guaranteed to enjoy more bliss in your lives.

ACCEPT YOUR LOVED ONE AS THEY ARE

Self-acceptance is a powerful tool you can use to enhance your self-love and self-esteem. In fact, it is one of the best things you can do for yourself.

Similarly, one of the best things you can do for your loved ones is to accept them exactly as they are. This doesn't mean you excuse their flaws or embrace their less-desirable qualities; it simply means that you see them for who they are and accept that reality, and you choose to be with them anyway.

Think about your loved one and all of her strengths and positive qualities. Cultivate gratitude for all the good things about your loved one and embrace a sense of appreciation for these traits. Write them down if that helps you to keep track of them and foster gratitude for each one.

Now, think about some of the funny or adorable little quirks about your loved one; maybe she always ends up burning dinner or she frequently forgets to pick up the dry cleaning. Think about how small those little faults are compared to their many positive qualities.

Realize that her flaws do not cancel out her positive qualities, nor do they highlight them; they simply are what they are.

Decide to accept your loved one as she is, flaws and faults and strengths included. Remind yourself that we all have our weak spots, and commit to not holding hers against her—as you expect she will not hold yours against you. It might take making the same decision many times over, but your feelings will follow your decision, especially if you act in a way that backs it up (e.g., not getting upset when she burns dinner or forgets the dry cleaning for the hundredth time).

Open yourself up to the bliss of having a loving relationship built on shared respect, trust, and honest acceptance of one another, and you won't regret it!

CREATE A LOVE TIME LINE

If you want a fun and creative activity you can do with your loved one to help you both find more bliss, creating a love time line is a great fit.

When you look back on a relationship, you can see it more clearly; you see the twists and turns you took to get where you are, and you can identify some high points on the journey.

Working with your partner, get out some paper and start a love time line. It should start with the moment you met and end with the current moment. You don't need to keep it a straight line—in fact, it should probably meander a bit, as your relationship experiences did!

Make sure to get all the important high points in there, like first date, first kiss, first "I love you," the moment you decided to move in together or get married, and any other vital moments in your relationship. Look back on your time together and enjoy the sense of bliss that arises from your efforts.

PROVIDE YOUR PARTNER WITH FEEDBACK

One of the best ways to ensure that a relationship is in a good place (and stays in a good place) is to communicate openly and honestly about the relationship.

You might feel like you have trouble getting your partner to open up about things like this, but you always have the option of setting the tone yourself!

Take 5 minutes to think about how your relationship is going, what is working well, what isn't, and what can be done to improve it. Come up with some bullet points on your own, then share them with your partner.

When you share these bullet points with your partner, keep the tone light and friendly, and assure her that you are not digging for flaws; you just want to make your relationship even better. This will make her more likely to agree to have the conversation and open up about her thoughts and feelings as well.

A couple that communicates well is able to find more joy in one another, so don't waste any more time avoiding this exercise—give it a try!

WORK ON YOUR SELF-LOVE IN ORDER TO LOVE OTHERS BETTER

Who is the most important person you are in a relationship with?

This is kind of a sneaky question, because most people will probably answer with their spouse, their child(ren), or another person who is near and dear to them. The answer, however, is much simpler: yourself!

The most important relationship you have with anyone on this earth is no doubt the one you cultivate with yourself. It is through your relationship with yourself that you connect to others, relate to others, and enjoy your time with others.

To work on your own self-love, try these suggestions:

- Block out self-deprecating thoughts when they pop into your head or shut them down with evidence that they are untrue.
- Keep your mind on your positive traits, your strengths, and things you are proud of accomplishing or engaging in.
- Forgive yourself for the mistakes you make and tell yourself that you love yourself—literally tell yourself that in the mirror.
- Practice good self-care. You will feel more positive about yourself and your body when you take good care of them. Make sure you are getting proper nutrition, sleep, and exercise, and try some healthy and fun activities.

- Set boundaries and say no to activities or people who deplete you physically or mentally.

Once you have a healthy sense of self-love and self-esteem, you will find it much easier to experience bliss in your relationships with others.

DETERMINE YOUR LOVE LANGUAGE

You've probably heard of Gary Chapman's book *The 5 Love Languages* from the 1990s. In case you haven't heard of it, it was written by a relationship expert about the five distinct ways we show our love for others and the ways we *want* others to show us love.

The five "Love Languages" are:

- Words of Affirmation
- Acts of Service
- Receiving Gifts
- Quality Time
- Physical Touch

Each of us has a primary love language that we "speak," and it's vital to understand what it is so we can improve our connections with others.

Read the book, go to the website (www.5lovelanguages.com/), or take a short quiz to discover what your primary language is and use that knowledge to let others know how to best show their love and appreciation. At the same time, think about what a loved one's primary language is, and try to cater your expressions of affection to match their language.

This relatively simple activity won't take more than a few minutes, but it can have a substantial impact on the quality of your relationships and enable you to find more bliss in each of them.

SPEND SOME TIME ALONE

It might seem counterintuitive, but spending time alone really is one of the healthiest things you can do for your relationships with others.

Spending time alone not only allows you to think, brainstorm, problem-solve, and simply space out and relax for a bit; it also helps you get to know yourself better—and you can only have a deep, meaningful, and satisfying relationship with someone else when you have a deep, meaningful, and satisfying relationship with yourself!

Take a few minutes each day to be by yourself. This is especially important if you live with and spend a lot of time with one or more of the people you love. The romantic ideal may be to spend every waking moment with someone you love, but the reality is not only impractical—it's also not very appealing! We all need a little alone time to reset, readjust, and get reacquainted with ourselves.

Use this alone time to think about what you want, assess your current state and well-being, and determine what is working well for you and what isn't.

Take what you learned back into your life and implement it to add some bliss to all your relationships.

PART 4
EXPERIENCE BLISS IN YOUR SURROUNDINGS

TAKE A MINDFUL WALK TO OBSERVE YOUR SURROUNDINGS

Everyone knows that taking a walk is good for your health, but you can also use a simple walk to boost your mood and improve your mental health!

Take 5 minutes to go on a short walk. You only have 5 minutes, so don't worry about planning where to go; just take a stroll around your block or up and down your street.

While you walk, challenge yourself to stay mindful of your surroundings. Look around you instead of keeping your gaze fixed straight ahead. Keep your mind open and observant of everything going on—what you pass, what you see, what you hear, what you feel, and the thoughts that pop in and out of your head. Make sure your breath is coming in and out at an even, measured pace and that you are mindful of each step you take.

For example:

1. **Begin your walk at a natural pace.** While staying aware of your surroundings for safety's sake, try to focus your attention on the sensation of walking. Notice the movement of your feet, the shifting of your body weight, and your breath as it leaves your body.
2. **Next, for a few minutes, pay attention to the sounds you hear.** Don't try to indentify the sounds; just notice them.

3. **Then focus on your sense of smell.** What scents do you notice on your walk?
4. **Now focus on what you can see.** Notice the colors, shapes, and objects all round you.
5. **As your walk comes to an end, focus on the sensation of walking again.** Feel your feet touching the ground; feel the vibration in your legs.
6. **Most important of all:** remember to enjoy your mindful walk and all the fresh air!

FIND THREE GOOD THINGS AROUND YOU

To become happier and more blissful, you can work on becoming more aware and appreciative of your surroundings. To become more aware and appreciative of your surroundings, try the simple exercise of finding three "good things" around you.

Look at your surroundings and identify at least three things that are beautiful, that make you happy, that are life-giving or life-enhancing, or that you simply enjoy looking at. You might pick out something as simple as a leaf or as complex as a person who is near and dear to you.

Think about each of these three things in turn, noting what it is that you love about it and why it is one of your three good things. Allow your heart to fill with gratitude and take delight in your three things.

If it feels natural to you, you can even thank each of these three things for the happiness they bring to you.

CULTIVATE APPRECIATION FOR YOUR HOME

It's easy to be happy when you remember to be cognizant and appreciative of all the good things in your life. One of the best things you have to be grateful for is the place you call home. Whether you own a house, rent an apartment, share a place with a roomie, or live with your family, you have something to be grateful for: a roof over your head and a place to shelter you from the hot sun, cold wind, and chilling rain.

Even if your living situation is not ideal, it's not hard to appreciate the very basic but life-changing advantages you enjoy when you have a place to live. You have a place to sleep, a place to get clean, a place to sit and relax at the end of your day, and a place to go when you just want to be "home."

Put together a list of all the benefits of living in your home. Write down those already mentioned if you need help getting started. Use this list to remember how wonderful it is to simply have a place to call home!

LOOK AT OLD PHOTO ALBUMS

As we grow older, we tend to forget that we've done quite a bit of growing and changing since our youth. Acknowledging that the only constant is change can help us to better understand ourselves and our journey, to boost our appreciation for everything we have, and to simply be happier and healthier!

If this sounds like a good idea for you, all you need to do is pull out some old photo albums. Spend a few minutes looking back at yourself at several different ages.

If you have baby pictures, check out a couple of those. See if you can find some old elementary school and middle school pictures, and check to see if you have any yearbooks from high school.

Look at photos from your childhood all the way up to the last few years and think about how much you have changed. Think about the knowledge, skills, and experience you have now.

Finish this exercise off by taking a picture of yourself right now. Now you'll have a new picture to add to your time line!

LOOK OUTSIDE TO FIND BLISS INSIDE

One of the best ways to rediscover bliss and excitement in your home is to appreciate it for the shelter it provides you from the elements. This exercise will make you extra grateful for your comfy home and help you appreciate the good parts of the worst weather.

When you find yourself disappointed to be stuck inside on a snowy day or trapped in the air-conditioned house on a sweltering day, take a moment to look outside. Look at the world outside and notice all the good and bad things outside your window.

For example, if it's snowy, think about how cold the snow is, how damp and chilly you would be if you were outside without (several!) warm layers on, and how the wind would quickly chap your face and hands.

Think about how wonderful it is that you have shelter that offers you safety and peace when there is a storm outside. You'll find it easy to be grateful that you are inside, all cozy and warm, while you appreciate the *good* parts of this weather: the sheen of sunshine or moonlight on the snow, the beauty of falling flakes, and the peace and tranquility of snow-covered trees.

If it's swelteringly hot outside, think about how sweaty and over-heated you would feel if you were stuck out there. Consider the sunburn you might get out in sun with no protection, and how uncomfortable or even dangerous it could be to be outside for too long.

Think about how great it feels to bask inside your house or apartment with its sweet, air-conditioned cool. If you have no AC at home, you can still be immensely grateful for the roof that is protecting you from the sun and the refrigerator that is providing ice and cold water to keep you cool. Revel in your comfortable environment and allow yourself to enjoy the positive parts of hot weather: the sunshine filtering through the trees, the sunlight providing plants with the energy they need to grow, the feel of sun-kissed (but not burned) skin.

One of the keys to bliss is enjoying and appreciating what you have—something that is easy to do when you're comfortable and cozy inside on a day with snowstorms or scorching temperatures!

STOP AND LISTEN

To enhance your happiness and appreciation for your surroundings, try this easy exercise. All you need to do is press the metaphorical "pause" button and listen.

We so often find ourselves tuning out our surroundings and spending time inside our heads. There's nothing wrong with some introspection, but it's good to make sure you get out of your head sometimes.

So, press that pause button on everything going on inside your head and be present. Listen to the sounds that are all around you. Notice those sounds that you were tuning out before. You might be surprised by how many sounds there are and how good you are at tuning them out!

As you identify all the sounds you hadn't heard before, think about how much you miss when going through life on autopilot. Think of all the beautiful things you might hear if you opened yourself up to them more often. Be grateful for your ability to hear all these sounds.

After a few minutes, press the "play" button and get back to your usual routine, but carry that gratitude and appreciation with you.

PLAN A PICNIC

If you don't quite have the time to go on a fun and relaxing picnic, try just planning one instead. Planning a fun experience can give you almost the same enjoyment as living it, or at least some of that enjoyment.

When you make your plan, think about all the important aspects of your picnic:

- **The place:** Where do you want to enjoy the outdoors? A park is a popular place for a picnic, but there are also busier or more isolated places you might like to visit.
- **The food:** What kind of food are you planning on taking? Do you have a theme or are you simply taking your favorite foods?
- **The guests:** Who will join you on this outing? Do you want to go solo, bring a significant other, or maybe invite a few close friends?
- **Games and fun:** Try planning a picnic scavenger hunt, or simply bring some balls, bats, Frisbees, or bocce balls for some outdoor fun.
- **The time:** Sure, most picnics take place around lunchtime, but there's no rule that says you can't have a breakfast picnic or a sunset picnic! Be creative and have fun.

Once you have all the specifics figured out, sit back and envision how much fun you'll have on your picnic. Think about how good it will feel to spend some time out in nature with some good food, good friends, and maybe a good glass of wine or two—if that's your thing!

PLAN A NATURE HIKE

You probably can't fit in a whole nature hike in 5 minutes, but you can plan a hike and get some of the same benefits in a fraction of the time.

Sit down and think about how long of a hike you'd like to go on. Plan your hike by distance if that's your goal, or by time if you'd rather take a more leisurely stroll.

Consider what scenery would be the most refreshing and invigorating for you. You might want to plan a more energizing hike along a busy road, or you may prefer a more secluded walk through the woods. If you have any hiking trails in your area that feature a pond, lake, or stream, you can plan your trail along the water to get a sense of calm and peace.

You can even print out a map of the area and trace your proposed route to get a sense of what kind of experience your hike will be. If you really want to approach some of the major benefits you get from hiking, try visualizing going on the hike you plan.

STAND IN THE RAIN

Remember when you were a kid and you loved the rain? Maybe you still love it now, but there's something special about rain for children.

To recapture that sense of wonder and joy that can come from a simple rainy day, follow these three steps:

1. **Look out the door or window at the rain.** Let the rain's calming effect wash over you, and follow your thoughts wherever they go (e.g., hot soup, curling up in a window seat with a good book, playing games inside on a rainy day when you were young).
2. **Go outside and stand in the rain—without an umbrella!** You won't be outside for long, but you'll need to feel the rain on your skin. Tilt your face up to the sky and hold your arms out, palms up, to feel the raindrops.
3. **Spend a minute or so just standing in the rain, appreciating the feel of it.** Allow it to refresh and renew you, and focus on the cleansing, rejuvenating aspect of standing in the rain.

When you go back inside, try to carry that clean and happy feeling along with you.

SOAK IN THE SUN

This exercise is particularly helpful for those who live in gray, cloudy, misty, or cool climates. It's much easier to appreciate the sun when you don't see it very often! However, anyone can engage in this exercise, no matter what climate they live in—as long as there's at least some sun to soak in!

On a sunny day, find a spot to sit or stand outside for a moment. Make sure you have at least some skin exposed to get that feel-good dose of vitamin D. Get comfortable in your seat or relax into a comfortable standing posture and tilt your face up toward the sun.

Feel the warmth on your face. Open yourself up to the sensation of soaking in energy and vitality from the sun. Visualize your body using that energy to heal you, protect you, and invigorate you.

The sun is your friend, but you should still lather up with a bit of SPF to protect your skin from the sun. It's especially important if you're very fair-skinned.

EXPERIENCE THE BREEZE

The breeze is an underappreciated part of nature. We rarely notice it unless it's *too* breezy or it's blowing our hair, napkin, or papers around! But if we take a moment to experience the breeze, we'll find that it really is something to appreciate.

It's a rare day that there is absolutely no breeze, so you should be able to do this at any time. Go outside and find a place to sit or stand and just be still. Close your eyes and take a moment to focus on what you hear. Is the breeze blowing through the trees, rustling leaves, or making that peculiar hollow noise as it passes over your ears?

Pay attention to how it feels. Notice the cool breeze on your face, the way it lifts the hair on your head and tickles the hair on your arms or legs.

Think about how nice it is to feel a breeze on a hot day and be thankful for the breeze and its gentle, cooling presence.

WALK A SHELTER DOG

Even if you have your own beloved dog to snuggle with, there are good reasons to give this exercise a try, including:

1. You get to branch out and make a new furry friend.
2. Your new furry friend gets a much-needed walk and some friendly human time.
3. The likely overworked and under-resourced staff at the shelter will appreciate your generosity.
4. You might make a new *best* furry friend! Who knows—you might fall in love and want to take your new buddy home with you.

If you've never walked a shelter dog before, don't worry! Shelter staff are always happy to get whatever help they can, and the worst that can happen is that they say no. They can also help you pick out the right dog for your temperament to ensure a pleasant walk.

When you take your rent-a-pup out on the trail, remember to stay mindful of what you're doing, how you're feeling, and how the dog seems to be feeling. Focus on the warm, fuzzy sensation of knowing you are doing a good deed and soak in the love and excitement you'll see in the dog's eyes. Keep that happy face at the forefront of your mind, and you'll find that you don't regret the time investment one bit.

If you're not really a dog person, there are alternate versions of this exercise you can try. For example, you could volunteer to sit with the shelter cats or help feed a new litter of kittens.

If you're not really an animal person, you could volunteer to do a non-animal-adjacent task at the shelter or find an entirely different nonprofit to spend some time volunteering with. Whatever activity you choose, the important thing is to do something good for someone else (human or animal!), stay mindful of your motivation and your experience, and do your best to enjoy your time well spent.

TIDY UP YOUR SPACE

Having a tidy and organized space can do wonders for your sense of peace and contentment. Of course, some people seem to thrive on chaos, but even if you're one of those types, you should be able to appreciate a small corner of neat, organized space!

Find one small space in your home that could use a bit of cleanup or organization and commit to 5 solid minutes of tidying. Use just three steps to do a quick tidy-up:

1. **Find items that need to be recycled or tossed out and sort them into these two categories.** Once you have everything sorted, take your loads to the garbage and recycle bins.
2. **Look for anything that belongs in another room, then separate and group these items by room.** Once you have everything separated by room, take the items that belong to the farthest room from you and put them back in their places. Repeat for every group.
3. **Arrange things in a way that you find visually appealing,** or go the easy route and just stick to right angles and keeping things parallel.

These three quick steps can give you a sense of relief and comfort in your space.

ENJOY A FIRE

There's something about a fire that draws the eyes to it like a magnet draws metal. Watching a fire burn can bring us peace, inspiration, and even bliss.

Harness these impressive properties of fire by giving yourself a chance to stare into the fire without distraction.

If you have a firepit or charcoal grill handy, prepare it for your fire. If you don't have a safe location for a fire nearby, surf your cable channel menu or look online for a video of a crackling fire. Most lineups with several channels have at least one option around the holidays, if not year-round.

Here's what to do:

1. Turn up the flames (real or fake) and give yourself a few minutes to simply sit and stare. Don't multitask by having it on in the background or cooking at the same time; just sit in silence and stare into the fire.
2. Observe the movement of the fire, the ever-changing colors, and the fluidity of the fire.
3. Listen to the crackling and popping of the fire.
4. If you are in front of a real fire, take a few deep breaths and smell the burning wood.

5. Feel the heat of the fire on your skin, and imagine that warmth radiating through your whole body filling you with warmth. Relax into that feeling.

6. Let the fire lull you into a blissful, relaxed state and allow your mind to wander where it will.

If you don't have any of the options previously mentioned, keep this exercise in your back pocket for the next time you go camping!

SIT IN SILENCE

We often forget how soothing and enjoyable it can be to simply sit in silence. This is partly because there is so little silence—there's always something buzzing, beeping, or blaring music and talking heads.

To find a little bit of bliss, try savoring the silence. Turn off the TV, silence your phone, switch off the radio, and see if you can find a quiet place away from anyone who might interrupt your few moments of peace and quiet.

When it's quiet, just sit for a few minutes. Drink in the silence, let it wash over you, and absorb it. Think about how great it is to hear absolutely nothing!

After a few moments, you might notice that you are more attentive to even the smallest sounds: the soft tick of the clock, the purring of your refrigerator, the small *whoosh* sound of your heat or AC kicking on. Cultivate gratitude for your sense of hearing and the wonderful things your ears allow you to hear: your child's laughter, your favorite song, the sound of birds chirping on a spring morning.

Keep that mindfulness with you as you go on about your day.

DO A WHIRLWIND CLEANING SESSION

There's nothing like the feeling of having a clean and organized living space. It's a task we rarely look forward to doing, but we always feel better once it's done!

You know that one spot in your home that always seems to attract dirt and dust? Perhaps it's the entryway, the laundry room, or the most frequented bathroom.

Wherever that spot is, take 5 minutes to do a "whirlwind clean." Grab a broom and do a quick sweep of the immediate area, aiming to just get the big stuff. Get out your duster or a damp washcloth and give all surfaces a little wipe-down. Finish off by cleaning up any cobwebs in the corners or tackling a couple of muddy spots on the floor with a paper towel and some good cleaner.

Allow yourself to feel the pleasure of tackling a few of the most obvious cleaning concerns. You don't need to deep-clean your whole house to feel a little boost of happiness or make your home feel a bit brighter; sometimes all that's necessary is a whirlwind clean!

MAKE A QUICK MEAL

Food is a surefire way to boost your mood, especially when it's something really delicious! To harness that mood boost, fire up the microwave or heat up the frying pan and whip up a quick bite to eat.

You get bonus mood points if your food smells super good while it cooks—think fragrant herbs, the smell of cookies baking, or the scent of garlic browning.

Follow these suggestions to take your experience to the next level:

- While you're cooking, pay attention to each step of the process; the process is likely a lot more detailed than it seems to you!
- Cultivate gratitude for your ability to engage in each of these steps.
- Drink in the sights, sounds, and smells throughout the cooking process. Let the experience put a smile on your face!
- Pat yourself on the back for making a delicious meal instead of buying one and sit down to enjoy your food.

ENJOY A PLEASANT SCENT

Your sense of smell is such a powerful tool. More than any other sense, your sense of smell is intimately tied to your memories. When you smell something uniquely associated with a past experience, you are transported back to that experience in an instant—something that simply doesn't happen as quickly or as intensely when you hear an associated sound or see an associated sight.

If you're looking for a little boost of happiness, take advantage of this huge mood influencer by simply smelling something good. It might be a candle, an air freshener, a specific dish, or even a scent that most people wouldn't find pleasant to smell but that is personally meaningful to you, like the smell of engine oil that reminds you of working on the car with your dad or the scent of a specific type of cleaner your grandmother always used.

Having trouble finding a pleasant scent from your past? You can also try one of these scents that have been proven to boost moods:

- Lemon
- Lavender
- Jasmine
- Rosemary
- Cinnamon
- Peppermint

Light the candle, spray the air freshener, or find some other way to enjoy the scent for a few minutes. Let your mind wander back to any good memories you have associated with the smell or, if it's simply a smell you enjoy, let yourself soak in the pleasant aroma.

CLEAN OUT YOUR CLOSET

I know, I know—cleaning out the closet is no one's idea of a good time, but it can be a very rewarding experience, in terms of both the actual outcome and how it can make you feel!

Since most of us have closets packed so full with clothes, shoes, and other belongings that it might take a full day to truly clean them out, we'll do a modified, quick-start version for now.

Take two large (and I mean *large*) garbage bags—one white and one black if you have them—and head on over to your closet. The white bag will be your donation bag and the black one your trash bag.

Now, with an alarm set for only 5 minutes, quickly go through the clothes and shoes cluttering up the closet and do one of three things with them:

1. Leave them where they are (keep them).
2. Fold them and put them in the white bag (donate them).
3. Throw them in the black bag (toss them).

Try to make split-second decisions; if you haven't worn something in ages, if it doesn't fit you, or if you just don't like the look of it anymore, take it out. Anything that's not too worn, ripped, or stained should go in the white bag, but anything that's a little worse for wear should go in the black bag.

Get through as much as you can in 5 minutes, then stop. If your bags aren't full and you have more to go through, you can always come back to this task for another quick cleanup session later on.

Take a moment to breathe a sigh of relief knowing that your closet is just a bit more organized and less cluttered than before. Enjoy that feeling!

For an extra boost of satisfaction, pick out the charity to which you plan to donate your old clothing and find a drop-box or drop-off location to recycle your old, too-worn clothes.

DO A 360-DEGREE SCAN

It's easy to get so wrapped up in your own little world that you forget to look around. That's a shame, because just looking around can have a huge impact on your happiness and your general outlook! To take advantage of this simple truth, try a 360-degree scan.

Wherever you are sitting or standing right now, make some space so you can turn in a complete circle. Stay where you are for now and take some time to get into a mindful state. Close your eyes, take three slow, deep breaths, and practice being present and staying in the moment.

When you feel ready, open your eyes and continue to practice staying mindful and aware. Turn to one side slowly and purposefully, scanning your surroundings as you do so. Keep turning and observing what is around you until you reach your starting point.

Now, back in your original position, think about all the things you saw that you wouldn't have seen otherwise. Thank yourself for taking a moment to look up and appreciate the beauty of the world around you.

TAKE A DIFFERENT WAY HOME

Humans are creatures of habit, but our tendency to stick to routine is not always to our benefit. To break the cycle of monotonous routine and inject a little bit of fun and novelty into your life, take one small action: find a different way home from work or school.

Don't type your address into your navigator or map out your route before you go; simply take a different turn than usual on your drive home, creating a small detour for yourself. When you're on the detour, take note of all the ways it differs from your usual drive.

Do you see more nature or less nature? More people or fewer people? A richer set of colors in the trees and bushes on the side of the road? Or perhaps there's not much of a difference at all, which is interesting in and of itself!

Your usual way home might be the most time-efficient, but how important are those few minutes if you rob yourself of the opportunity to think outside the box? Do yourself a favor and take a new way home.

PLAN (OR MAKE) A FUN NEW PURCHASE

Retail therapy is NOT a good long-term option for enhancing your happiness, but a small, well-deserved gift for yourself every now and then can make the difference between "doing fine" and "doing great!"

Think about something you really want—not something you need, just something you *want*. It should be something fun, unnecessary, and not too terribly expensive; think a fancy new pillow, a kitchen accessory, or a tool that will make your life just a little bit easier. Try to align it with your values and interests (e.g., go for the kitchen accessory if you're a big foodie or an avid recipe experimenter).

Once you have figured out what you want to treat yourself with, you have two options:

1. Find out where this item is sold and plan when you'll go to buy it.
2. Find this item online and order it from your phone or laptop.

Option 1 is the better one because you get to make a whole experience out of treating yourself, but Option 2 can be super convenient if the store that sells it is far away or if its hours do not match your schedule.

Whichever option you take, enjoy your fun new purchase!

TAKE ADVANTAGE OF YOUR SURROUNDINGS

If you find yourself sticking to routine and hesitating to try new things, or if you're a homebody who rarely gets out for fun, this is a great exercise to try.

Spend a few minutes thinking about your neighborhood. What is nearby your house or apartment? Are there restaurants just down the road? A thrift store across the street? A friendly next-door neighbor whom you haven't engaged with very often? Perhaps an indoor water park, specialty grocery store, or gym within a few blocks?

Whatever you come up with, pick one spot and commit to taking advantage of your proximity. If you choose a nearby restaurant, plan to go check it out for dinner.

If you choose a thrift store, make plans to stop by after work one day.

If you choose the friendly neighbor, make some cookies or another treat you are good at whipping up and take it to him or her to start up some conversation.

It's silly that we often don't take advantage of the opportunities that are right in front of us. This exercise is one of the most low-effort ways to engage your curiosity and keep yourself open-minded and open-hearted.

CHANGE YOUR PERSPECTIVE

Do you have a favorite spot on the couch? Most of us do! It's our favorite for a reason—it's cozy, it probably has a good angle on the TV, and we're comfortable with the view of our surroundings from that position.

However, as comfy as it can be in our favorite spot, a lack of novel perspective in our *physical* position can translate to a lack of *mental* perspective too. When you lack mental perspective, you can find it all too easy to lose sight of all the things that make you happy.

To counteract this loss, change it up by adjusting your physical perspective.

Instead of relaxing in your usual spot, get up and find another seat—in a chair, on the floor on a cushion, or even just at the other end of the couch. Wherever it is, the important thing is that you have a different view from this second spot.

Take a few moments to look around and notice what looks different from this angle. Consider how such a small tweak can sometimes make such a big difference and commit to remembering that when it comes to your inner perspective as well.

USE ONE OBJECT AROUND YOU

The title of this exercise might sound kind of funny—what's so special about using an object? What makes it an "exercise"? The part that makes this exercise a useful way to spend 5 minutes is the way you pick the object.

Wherever you are right now, look around you and pick one object. It should be:

- Something that you don't use very often (e.g., not your cell phone or laptop).
- Something with a very specific purpose (e.g., not a towel or a pen).
- Something that you might have forgotten you had!

If you're like most people, you've got at least a few things lying around the house that you bought with excitement, used only once or twice, then completely forget about. Maybe it's a foot spa, a massaging chair, or a foam roller. It might be an air popcorn popper, a food processor, or some other kitchen gadget that made you say, "Cool!" when you first saw it.

Whatever it is, drag it out of the closet or cupboard and use it. When you use it, remember how excited you were to buy it and use it. Consider how much money you spent on it and think about what that means in terms of how much you valued it. Try to get your money's worth out of the object by putting it to good use now.

If the object is a foot spa, fill that puppy up and soak your tootsies! If it's a massaging chair or a foam roller, get to releasing and relaxing those muscles! If it's a kitchen gadget or accessory, whip up something good to eat and make it a doubly effective exercise.

The point is to get some use out of a rarely used object. It will make you feel good about your purchase, give you an opportunity to try a new or rarely practiced activity, and remind you of how important it is to pay attention to the tools and opportunities all around you.

FIND A NEW, PEACEFUL SPOT TO REFLECT

Changing up your routine can have tons of positive outcomes, especially when you're open to making changes and trying new methods.

To make a positive change in your routine and open your mind to what's around you, choose a new spot to engage in some in-depth reflection. (If you're not sure how to get started with reflection, see the "Reflect On Your Life" exercise in Part 1.)

Wherever you usually reflect, think about what makes that spot so effective. Is it the comfort factor? The privacy? The smells, sights, and sounds? Note these factors.

Now, find a spot that is the exact opposite of your usual spot. If you usually reflect in private, choose a public place. If you prefer to be in your favorite comfy chair, choose a park bench or hard surface to sit on.

In your new spot, try reflecting in the same way you usually do. You'll probably find that it's a bit of a different experience, which is the point! Enjoy the novelty and try to apply that "outside the box" thinking to your reflection, enhancing your experience and bringing you bliss.

GET LOST, FIND YOURSELF

It's usually not a great feeling to get lost, but it all depends on your perspective. If you're an adventurous soul, or if you'd like to work on being more adventurous, try getting lost!

Now, you don't need to get well and truly lost for this exercise to benefit you. All you need to do is get a taste.

When going for a walk, a run, a hike, or even a drive, make it a point to go somewhere new and unfamiliar. Get out of your comfort zone (but stay safe, of course).

Challenge yourself to explore this new area without checking your phone or using your GPS. Simply enjoy the feeling of being in a new place and cultivate your sense of adventure by getting just a little bit lost.

It can be a surprisingly enjoyable experience, but it can also help you get to know yourself better and bring you the joy of getting in touch with the inner "you."

REMOVE YOURSELF FROM THE SITUATION

Sometimes all you need to find a little joy is to remove yourself from whatever situation you are currently in—even if it's not a particularly bad situation!

If you find yourself lacking joy and stuck in a stagnant situation, whether it's comfortable and familiar or stifling and unpleasant, just remove yourself. It's best if you *physically* remove yourself from the situation, but you can always practice some meditation or visualization to remove yourself mentally if physically leaving the area isn't an option.

The important part is to get your mind off your current environment and mix things up a bit. Go somewhere else, do something else, think about something else—whatever it takes to get completely removed from the stagnant situation.

Give yourself some bonus bliss points by engaging in something completely new and maybe even a little bit nerve-racking for you, like going to a social club or organization without knowing anyone or trying a brand-new hobby without any background or experience in it. Be new! Be bold! You'll thank yourself for it later.

FIND A MEMORY

Our minds are rich and complex, full of mysterious processes and unknown connections. Learning more about ourselves is a challenge, but it is one that is immensely enjoyable and fulfilling.

To learn a bit more about yourself and find joy in your surroundings, practice "finding a memory."

Here's how to do it:

1. Look around the room you are in and take a brief mental inventory of the objects within it (e.g., table, tablecloth, two chairs, framed photograph, end table, snow globe, lamp).
2. Rack your brain for a good memory that is connected to one of these items. Try to think of something that involved a loved one and/or that resulted in shared love and laughter (e.g., when your brother's dog knocked over the lamp at the worst possible moment, or when your friend brought you the snow globe as a meaningful gift).
3. Replay this entire memory in your head from start to finish.

You will likely find a smile on your face as you finish reliving the memory. Enjoy the smile, cherish the memory, and continue on through your day with just a bit more bliss.

END YOUR HIKE WITH A MINDFUL MOMENT

If you're the kind of person who lives for hiking and spending time in nature, this is a great exercise for you to try. You can tack it on to the end of just about any hike or outdoor adventure, and it only takes a few minutes to complete.

Toward the end of your hike (or at a particularly beautiful spot along the way), stop and take a few minutes to be mindful. Take in the scenery around you and appreciate the beauty of nature.

Next, close your eyes and take a deep breath in through your nose. Smell all the scents of nature and try to identify them (e.g., pine trees, sap, rain).

Keep your eyes closed and listen to all the sounds of nature. Try to identify them as well (e.g., bird chirping, wind rustling the leaves, a babbling brook).

Open your eyes and take another minute or two to simply "be." Focus on appreciating where you are and how you got there.

Try to carry that sense of bliss and mindful awareness with you as you end your hike and go about your business.

STARE AT THE STARS

There's nothing better at making us feel small than looking up at the stars. Although feeling small might not *sound* like a blissful experience, it certainly can be in this context.

Wait until the sky is as dark as it gets in your area—or better yet, take a short trip to somewhere with an even clearer view. It's amazing how much clearer the sky is and how much brighter the stars are away from cities and towns.

Lay down a blanket, set up a chair, or simply stand and stare straight up at the sky.

Look at all the stars and think about how many more stars there are that we simply can't see. Take a moment to appreciate the vastness of our universe and imagine how many other solar systems and planets like ours are out there.

As you revel in the beauty of the stars, try this quick meditation:

- Relax your body and close your eyes for a moment.
- When you open them back up, try to take in the vastness of the night sky. Let your vision be broad and look at the stars without thinking of them specifically or any preconceived notions you have about them, like which ones make up which constellations; instead, just be open to the vastness of the sky and the universe.

- Think about how lucky you are to be *where* you are, *when* you are, and *how* you are: able to look up at the sky and engage your imagination.
- Let the stars make you feel small and slight, and revel in the feeling that you are a tiny part of something so much bigger than you.

GO CLOUD-WATCHING

Remember when you were young and you would stare up at the clouds, seeing interesting shapes and exotic animals prancing across the sky? There was nothing better than lying back in the grass and watching as they drifted by, pointing out the interesting ones to your friends.

Relive that blissful feeling by finding a good, grassy spot to lie down and fix your eyes on the sky. Watch as the clouds drift slowly by and try to come up with something that each distinct cloud reminds you of—an animal, a face, a sailboat, or anything else your mind comes up with. Side note: keep in mind that a hammock makes for an excellent addition to this exercise.

Cloud-watching is an excellent way to practice creativity and use your imagination, but people generally don't really do it after they become adults and start shouldering adult responsibilities.

This is too bad, because adults need that boost of creativity and imagination more than ever! Challenge your imagination and find shapes in the sky to get a childlike sense of bliss in your surroundings.

REORGANIZE ONE ROOM

Sometimes all you need to get your daily dose of bliss is to shake things up a bit. One way to do this is by reorganizing a room in your home. You don't need to buy all new furniture or paint the walls to make a room feel fresh and new; all you need to do is move things around.

Here's how to go about it:

1. Pick a room you'd like to reorganize; it should be one you spend a good deal of time in, like your living room or bedroom.
2. Look around the room and find at least two or three largish items that you can feasibly move yourself.
3. Plan out the room's new look or at least a couple of possibilities for the room's new look.
4. Get to work! It shouldn't take long if you already have the plan in mind.

Once you have finished reorganizing the room, stop and survey your work. What do you think of the new look? If you like it, keep it! If not, put everything back the way it was and thank yourself for the mini workout!

FLOAT TO FIND BLISS

There's not much in this life that's more blissful than floating on top of a slow-moving river or gently lapping lake. Whether you're staring up at blue sky or closing your eyes in bliss, floating is a great feeling!

To capture a bit of that bliss when you're out and about near the water, set aside a few minutes to simply float uninterrupted. Look up and appreciate the blue sky, count the puffy clouds, or keep your eyes shut and your ears open to the beautiful sounds of nature all around you.

It might sound like a cliché, but there's one more thing you can do to maximize your bliss as you float—take a deep breath in through your nose and let it out in one big sigh. A happy and contented sigh can make you feel even more relaxed and enhance your enjoyment of the situation.

If you're not near a body of water large enough to float on, you may want to check out a sensory deprivation tank instead. In one of those you can shut down all your sense and focus completely on feeling blissful!

PLAY HIDE-AND-SEEK

If you want to get more familiar with an area, see places you don't usually see, and have some fun all at the same time, hide-and-seek is the activity for you!

Grab a couple friends or invite a few of the children in your life to join you (with their parents' permission, of course) and explain the rules of the game if they don't know them already:

- There is one seeker who must keep his eyes closed and count to thirty before opening them.
- The rest of the players must hide from the seeker.
- Whomever the seeker finds first is the next seeker, but the game can continue until the current seeker has found all hiders.
- Before the new seeker begins seeking, all hiders must rejoin the group and start from the same place.

Tell the players that the goal of this game is to get to know the area better and appreciate what is around them. Keep this in mind for yourself too.

As you play, make note of any interesting, odd, or potentially useful things in your surroundings. Enjoy exploring and allow the game to bring you a little taste of childhood joy.

CULTIVATE CHILDLIKE WONDER

If you've given many of the other exercises in this book a try, you'll notice that a lot of them are drawn from things we do as children. There's a good reason for this: as children, we are generally much more open to bliss.

With adulthood comes more responsibility, less excitement, and more "contentment" rather than bliss. This is normal, but we don't need to give up on feeling that sense of awe and bliss that is so easily accessible when we are children!

To open yourself up to greater bliss and enjoyment of the world around you, work on cultivating a childlike sense of wonder.

Here's how: look around you and see everything as if it's the first time you've ever seen it. Do your best to see it in a new light, shedding your preconceived notions and prior knowledge of its function or how it works.

Here are a few ideas about how to apply some of that wonder to your everyday adult life:

- **Learn something new.** Learning is one of the top ways to promote wonder. Try reading a book, watching a documentary or TV show, or even watching an online tutorial on something you've always been fascinated by. Think about what topics make you happy or something you've always wanted to know about and go to it!

- **Try photography.** Sometimes the simple act of capturing the beauty of something on film can produce an amazing sense of wonder about both the object and the world.
- **Watch kids.** When it comes to looking at the world with wonder, kids know how to do it right. There is an excitement to everyday things for children that we lose as adults, so try taking 5 minutes to watch the wonder in a child; it will open up the same feelings in you.

Go out and find delight in the smallest things, like seeing Christmas lights or spying a bunny out in the woods. Open yourself up to childlike wonder, and bliss will surely follow!

LOOK INTO THE PAST

A fun exercise to keep an open mind and get a new perspective is to "look into the past." This doesn't mean you actually crack open a history book; rather, it means that you look around yourself and imagine your surroundings as they were at some point in the past.

The exact point is up to you; you could choose to look back a year, twenty years, one hundred years, or even 1,000 years into the past.

After you choose your point in time, take a good, long look around you. Think about how different things might have looked. Think about what things you are grateful for right now that would not be there at your point in the past. Consider what life would have been like in this place at that point in time, and cultivate gratitude for living where and when you do!

Opening a small personal window into the past can help you appreciate what you have now, fire up your imagination about the past, and encourage you to think outside the box and learn new things. All of these potential outcomes can be strong contributors to bliss, so don't wait—get started looking into the past!

PEER INTO THE FUTURE

Like the previous "Look Into the Past" exercise, this exercise does not require you to actually be able to see into the future; all you have to do is use your imagination and let your creativity run just a little bit wild.

Stop and look around you. Think about all the things in the room or area, what the purpose of the area is, and what it is currently used for.

Once you have some answers in mind, start thinking about the future of this area. Decide on a point in the future (e.g., ten years, twenty years, one hundred years) and ask yourself:

- What will this area be used for at that point in time?
- What kinds of structures, furniture, or tools will be here?
- How will people feel when they walk through this area? What will they be doing or on their way to doing?

Engage the creative side of your brain and come up with some possible answers. It doesn't matter if they are even remotely realistic, since the point of the exercise is to expand your mindset, think about the future, and find some bliss in your current circumstances.

LET YOUR IMAGINATION RUN WILD

If you want to truly reach out and grab as much bliss as you can, this exercise is a great option. Your imagination is a precious thing; it can lead you to innovation and ingenuity, entertain you, encourage you, distract you, and make you more joyful and spontaneous—all of which lead to greater bliss in your life.

To practice letting your imagination run wild, set aside a little bit of time and try these methods:

- Close your eyes for a couple of minutes and simply see where your brain takes you.
- Combine two disparate things to come up with something new, something bizarre, or something hilarious (e.g., notice a person walking their dog and a duck flying overhead, and combine the two to imagine a person walking a duck while a dog flies overhead).
- Think about the fictional concept that most excited and interested you as a kid; perhaps it was dragons or unicorns, witches and wizards, or the idea of animals being able to talk. Whatever it was, pour your energy into imagining your childhood interest as a reality.

PRACTICE FINDING HUMOR IN AN UNEXPECTED SITUATION

Humor is one of humanity's most effective tools to encourage joy and enhance bliss. It is at your disposal 24/7, although you may not always realize it.

To boost your bliss, practice finding humor when it is least expected. Follow these steps to give it a shot:

1. **When you want to feel more bliss, stop and look around you.** It's probably not a particularly wonderful environment if you are on the lookout for more bliss, but take in your surroundings anyway.
2. **Find something that could be a source of humor.** That might be a silly hat someone is wearing, a misspelling of "detail-oriented" in an email, or any other example of irony or humor.
3. **Embrace the humor!** Laugh at the silly or ironic thing you noticed and move on to the next bit of funny you can find.

The more you practice finding humor in all situations, the more able you will be to cultivate a sense of bliss anywhere, anytime.

ALTER YOUR SURROUNDINGS
TO BRING YOU BLISS

It's great to be able to find bliss in your surroundings, whether they are inherently bliss-inducing or not; however, sometimes your best option is to curate the right environment that will allow bliss to enter your life without too much effort.

To make your environment more conducive to experiencing bliss, follow these steps:

1. Look around you and notice anything that actively inhibits or saps away your bliss.
2. Think about *why* it is not conducive to bliss; is it simply not to your liking, or is it associated with something bigger?
3. If it's simply not to your liking, remove whatever it is from your environment. If it's associated with something bigger, take a few moments to explore that something.
4. Identify that larger "something" and determine what you can do in terms of altering your surroundings to make them more conducive to bliss.
5. Continue until there is nothing left around you that actively inhibits or hinders your bliss.

Of course, you can't remove *everything* from your life that does not contribute to bliss, but there's no harm in curating an effective bliss-boosting environment wherever you can!

PUT YOURSELF IN AN UNCOMFORTABLE SITUATION

Yes, it sounds counterintuitive! But the fact is that difficult, challenging, and uncomfortable situations are the only situations in which you grow, and you often find that bliss is tied to personal growth.

To give yourself more opportunities for personal growth, make it a point to put yourself in a brief uncomfortable situation.

Here are some suggestions if you're not sure where to start:

- Sign up to attend a networking event where you don't know anybody.
- Volunteer to present something important and complex at work.
- Ask someone to teach you something you have absolutely no understanding of.
- Introduce yourself to a stranger for no reason other than to get to know a stranger!

These are just a few of the many examples of situations that are uncomfortable for many people. If none of these sounds particularly uncomfortable, come up with your own uncomfortable scenarios and seek them out.

It will be hard, but remind yourself that this is the only way to grow, and personal growth leads directly to greater bliss.

GO SOMEPLACE WHERE YOU CAN FIND MEANING

Meaning is an elusive and sometimes downright slippery thing to hold on to; luckily, there are tons of ways you can find and build your own meaning. The more meaning you find in your everyday life, the more bliss you will experience.

Logically, enhancing your sense of meaning and purpose in life will also lead directly to greater bliss. To get a little boost of meaning and an indirect boost of bliss, try going somewhere that is meaningful to you or somewhere that makes it easy to find meaning.

This might be at your church down the street, at the organization where you volunteer on the weekends, or even just in your own garden at home.

Once you get there, open yourself up and allow that sense of meaning and purpose to fill you up. Notice the joy you feel when you give yourself to a greater purpose. Revel in that feeling of joy and thank yourself for making the trek—however long it was—to enhance the meaning and bliss in your life.

INSTITUTE A THREE-TO-ONE RULE

The three-to-one rule is a method for noticing and identifying at least three positive things for every one negative thing around you.

Sometimes this exercise is easy and sometimes it's not, but you'll find it gets easier the more you practice it. You'll also find yourself more open to bliss in your life as you shift your focus toward the positive.

Here's how to give the three-to-one rule a try:

1. Look around and identify the first "negative" thing that comes to mind (e.g., a dirty house, a rude customer, an annoying coworker).
2. Now look around and identify three "positive" things to counteract the one negative (e.g., the many pictures of your happy family on the fridge, three smiling customers, or three nice emails you have received).
3. Continue this process until you've found three good things for each negative thing you notice in the room.

Practicing the skill of finding three times the good relative to the bad will make you a more positive person overall and more attuned to the positive, which can bring you three times the bliss (or more)!

GO FOR A DRIVE

For many of us, driving is not an enjoyable task. It's an unfortunate part of living our everyday life, especially if we have a long or particularly arduous commute to work and back. However, driving *can* be an activity that is peaceful, soothing, and blissful.

To find bliss in a quick trip, take a few minutes to plot out a route that is "off the beaten trail" (or not one of your common routes), is not too busy, and has a relatively high speed limit (at least 45 or 50 mph).

When you go for your drive, try to keep your mind open to whatever thoughts want to pop up, but don't hold on to them too tightly—let them enter your mind and then gently fade away.

If it's not too cold, roll the windows down and feel the breeze. Turn the radio to a good station and lose yourself in the music. Watch the scenery pass by and be thankful for the ability to see so much in so little time.

Let yourself get into the groove of driving and allow yourself to feel the simple joy of a drive to nowhere in particular.

HONOR YOUR ENVIRONMENT

It's wonderful to cultivate appreciation and gratitude for our environment, but we can take it a step further. There's liking and being grateful for your environment, and there's *honoring* your environment; honoring your environment is one of the top levels of understanding and finding bliss in your life.

Instead of just walking down your street and thinking, "I love that willow tree" or "I'm so glad I live here," do something to make your environment even better. For example, can you:

- Pick up trash on the side of the road?
- Lend a hand with community events?
- Volunteer at the local fire department?
- Plant a native species in your garden?
- Pay more attention to how you use water and conserve where possible?
- Visit a national park and enjoy the scenery?
- Bike or walk to your destination instead of taking the car? (Extra points here for the exercise you'll get.)
- Create a compost pile for you own home or donate to a local composting program?

Whatever you have the time and/or money to do, make sure you are engaging in activities that not only show appreciation for the environment but also show that you honor and respect your environment and intend to leave it in the same state you found it—if not an even better one.

Find joy in honoring your environment and celebrate your commitment to making a better world.

PLAY IN A MOUND OF FALL LEAVES

Do you remember how great it felt to fall into a big pile of leaves and just sink to the bottom? Believe it or not, it's still that much fun!

As is the case with many of the things you enjoyed as a kid, it didn't become less fun as an adult—you just stopped doing it for one reason or another. It happens to almost all of us with time, but we can get it back.

All you have to do is go out and find a big pile of fall leaves and hop right in it! You may want to make sure it's *your* pile of leaves and not your neighbor's, unless you don't mind getting odd looks and having to clean up your neighbor's yard.

Kick it up a notch by running and jumping into the pile of leaves. As you sink into it, take a deep breath and recognize the scent of dry leaves. Hear the leaves crackle as you move around in the pile. And open your eyes to see the myriad of colors that make up fall leaves.

Open yourself up to the simple pleasure of playing in a pile of fall leaves.

BUILD A SNOWMAN

If it's too late for jumping in fall leaves (see the previous exercise), you might be able to try this exercise instead. Unleash your inner child and your inner artist all at once by creating a snowman that is authentically "you."

In case you forgot how, here's how to build a snowman:

1. Roll some snow into a ball and keep rolling it until it's big enough to be the base.
2. Roll a slightly smaller ball for the middle section.
3. Roll an even smaller ball of snow for the head.
4. Grab some coal or buttons for the eyes and mouth and make sure to get a carrot for the nose, a hat for the head, and a scarf to tie around the neck.

Of course, all these accoutrements are optional—if you want to make a snowman with dreadlocks instead of a top hat, go for it! If you prefer your snowman to be a perfect gentleman, go ahead and make him a monocle and pocket watch.

Use that creative snowman-building skill that has probably lain dormant since you were a child and feel the joy slowly suffuse you.

PICK SOME WILDFLOWERS

If you've missed out on both fall and winter, fret not! You can still engage in a fun springtime activity to find bliss in your surroundings.

Spring is the perfect time for gathering flowers, since this is when they are shooting up from the increased amount of sun and rain they are likely getting.

Take advantage of the season by searching for the closest meadow or field of wildflowers and making a quick trip to go collect some. If you have multiple options, go to the one with the type of flowers or color that you prefer.

Stay mindful of the beauty you are experiencing as you pick the flowers. Don't miss a single hue due to mindlessness, and be appreciative for each one you see.

Collect a good bunch of flowers and return home to display them on your dining room table or your kitchen counter—anywhere you will see them often. And don't forget to water them!

Let yourself envision that beautiful field every time you walk by them and warmly greet that sense of bliss that's knocking to come into your life.

CATCH A SUNRISE

If you're not a morning person, this is an excellent opportunity to try something new!

Getting up early and watching the sun rise is a great way to find bliss in your surroundings, and it can get your day off to a great start.

To find some sunrise bliss, get up at least 15 minutes before the sun rises. Check the local sunrise time to make sure you don't miss it. Pour yourself some coffee or tea, put on a comfy robe, and find a good spot to watch the sun come up.

Alternatively, you could find a good remote location to view the sunrise from, like the top of a nearby hill or over a beautiful lake. This will take a little more planning, but it can also bring you a greater dose of bliss.

You can also try doing a short meditation while watching the sunrise. For many people a meditation done at sunrise is more effective at reliving stress and promoting calm than meditation done later in the day. Perhaps it has something to do with the quite peacefulness of the sunrise; the world has not begun its hustle and bustle, and everything seems still and calm. Meditating at sunrise also puts you in a positive frame of mind, helps you handle what the day brings with less aggravation, and sets your day off on the right foot—and what could be more blissful than that?

As you watch the sun rise, think about how grateful you are to be able to experience it. You have eyes to see it and ears to hear any accompanying sound, like birds chirping or roosters crowing.

Drink in the sights and sounds and allow yourself to experience the bliss of watching a beautiful sunrise.

PRACTICE SUNSET MINDFULNESS

Each day you experience is an opportunity to live your life to the fullest, so why not end the day with some gratitude for all you have experienced, felt, and lived. To end your day with some gratitude and mental clarity, try a sunset mindfulness practice:

- **As you watch the colors change across the sky and the sun slide down toward the earth, let it bring to mind the inevitability of change.** Each day you face enormous change: from pitch-black night to bright and clear day, then back again. You also face the changing seasons as the year progresses. Change is an inevitable part of life, and sunsets help you remember that.
- **Remind yourself to feel grateful for the day that you were given** and to foster appreciation for the opportunities you had in this day.
- **Keep your attention on the sunset** and gently bring your thoughts back to it if you catch them wandering off.
- **Notice how time passes as you focus on the sun's gradual journey out of sight.** Note whether it feels fast, slow, or somewhere in between today. Think about what that means—if it feels slow, are you anxious to get off to your next appointment? If so, gently push that anxiety out of your mind. If it feels fast, are you hanging on too tightly to this one moment in time? If so, gently remind

yourself that the sun rises and sets each day, and that this is simply the natural order of things.

- **As the sun sinks low and eventually disappears, embrace the coming darkness as the inevitable progression after light,** as well as a precursor to the inevitable return of light.

Allow yourself to relax into your more natural state after the sun has set, then spend a minute or two thinking about how wonderful it is to be able to enjoy a sunset. Thank yourself for the opportunity, and offer up some gratitude to God, the universe, or whatever other entity you would like to thank.

INDEX

ABOUT THE AUTHOR

Courtney E. Ackerman, MA, is the author of *My Pocket Positivity*, a book that aims to help readers inject a little more positivity and happiness into their lives. Courtney's freelance work includes survey research design and consulting, and she is a regular contributor to the Positive Psychology Program, an organization that advocates for greater attention to and application of the tenets of positive psychology in the real world. She is also a researcher at a state agency focused on improving the access to and the quality of healthcare in California.

After earning a degree in psychology from the State University of New York at Oswego, Courtney made the move to Southern California to attend Claremont Graduate University. There, she earned a master's degree in positive organizational psychology and evaluation, a focus which helped her realize her niche: a research-based but purposefully practical perspective, somewhere on the spectrum between the objectivity of strict science and the approachability of pop psychology.

Courtney finds joy in helping people learn how to take advantage of research findings and apply them in their own lives. She is particularly interested in compassion, happiness and well-being at work, survey research, and positive psychology in general.

When she's not working, Courtney likes to spend time with her dog, explore the many nearby wineries and craft breweries, and soak in the beauty of Northern California's forests, lakes, and hiking trails. She is also an avid reader and enjoys doing nerdy things like watching science fiction and playing video games to relax and de-stress.

5 MINUTES
to a Better You!

PICK UP OR DOWNLOAD YOUR COPIES TODAY!